THE
OLD WEST TRIVIA
BOOK

By Don Bullis

The Old West Trivia Book
Copyright © 1993 Gem Guides Book Company
315 Cloverleaf Dr., Suite F
Baldwin Park, CA 91706

Cover Design: Kimura Bingham Graphic Design

Library of Congress Catalogue Number
ISBN 0-935182-62-4

Printed in the United States of America

Dedicated to Gloria Bullis, my partner
along the trails of the Old West.

TABLE OF CONTENTS

LAWMEN AND OTHER WHITE HAT GUYS

Some Were Better Than Others

CHAPTER 1

Q: What position of authority did Bat Masterson (1853-1921) hold in and around Dodge City, Kansas, in the late 1870s and early 1880s?

A: He was sheriff of Ford County from 1877 to 1881. Dodge City was the county seat.

———?ι———

Q: How did Sheriff Masterson come to be called "Bat"?

A: One source indicates that his name was Bartholomew, which was shortened to Bat. Another source reports his real name as Barclay, likewise shortened to Bat(?). Legend also holds that he was called Bat because he was such an excellent shot that he could kill a bat on the wing with a pistol.

———?ι———

Q: What ever became of Bat Masterson?

A: He became a sports writer for the New York City *Morning Telegraph*. He died at his desk of natural causes in 1921.

———?ι———

Q: What lawman was shot and killed on the south side of the railroad tracks in Dodge City by Kansas cowboys Jack Wagner and Alf Walker in April of 1878?

A: City Marshal Ed Masterson, Bat's older brother. Wagner was killed in the fight and Walker seriously injured.

———?————

Q: Who played Bat Masterson on the 1958-1961 TV series of the same name?

A: Gene Barry (1919- --).

———?————

Q: Perfecto Armijo was sheriff of Bernalillo County, New Mexico, in the late 1870s and early 1880s. He arrested a famous outlaw long before Sheriff Pat Garrett did. Who was the outlaw?

A: Billy the Kid. Sheriff Armijo arrested Billy in the spring of 1880 for an unspecified infraction. Sheriff Garrett didn't arrest Billy until December of 1880. (Billy escaped from the Bernalillo County jail in May of 1880.)

———?————

Q: Name the Kansas and Arizona lawman who had brothers named James, Morgan, Virgil and Warren.

A: Wyatt Earp (1848-1929).

———?————

Q: Who was the sheriff of Cochise County, Arizona, when Virgil Earp was town marshal in Tombstone?

A: John Behan was the first sheriff of Cochise County, appointed in 1881. He was sympathetic to the faction which opposed the Earp brothers and Doc Holliday at the O.K. Corral gunfight but he did not participate, though he was nearby.

———?————

Q: By what name was Georgian John Holliday better known?

A: "Doc" Holliday. Consumptive and alcoholic, he was a dentist by vocation and a gambler and killer by avocation. At 28 years of age he was wounded in the gunfight at the O.K. Corral on October 26, 1881. He died of tuberculosis at Denver six years later.

————?¿————

Q: A gunfight took place on October 26, 1881, on Fremont Street near the O.K. Corral in Tombstone, Arizona Territory. How long did it last?

A: By most accounts, it lasted less than one minute.

————?¿————

Q: How many casualties were there in the gunfight at O.K. Corral?

A: When the smoke cleared, Billy Clanton and brothers Tom and Frank McLaury were dead of multiple gunshot wounds. Doc Holliday and brothers Virgil and Morgan Earp were wounded. Of the eight participants, only Ike Clanton and Wyatt Earp were not injured.

————?¿————

Q: What legal action was taken against the Earp brothers and Holliday after the gunplay on Fremont Street in Tombstone?

A: Not much. Virgil was dismissed as Tombstone town marshal and Wyatt and Doc were arrested for murder by Sheriff John Behan. A local magistrate judge later ruled that the defendants were guilty of bad judgment but no criminal acts.

————?¿————

Q: Can you name the two contestants in a non-championship heavyweight boxing match refereed by Wyatt Earp in San Francisco, California, in 1896?

A: Bob Fitzsimmons and Tom Sharkey. Fitzsimmons knocked Sharkey down in the eighth round and Earp counted him out. Then he picked up Sharkey's hand and declared him the winner saying that Fitzsimmons had thrown an illegal punch. The word was out that the fix was in and Earp was a part of it.

―――――?ὶ―――――

Q: Can you name the actor who played Wyatt Earp in John Ford's 1946 movie, *My Darling Clementine*? Who played Doc Holliday?

A: Henry Fonda (1905-1982) played Wyatt and Victor Mature (1916- --) played Doc.

―――――?ὶ―――――

Q: Can you name the actor who played Wyatt Earp in John Sturges' 1957 movie, *Gunfight at the O.K. Corral*? Who played Doc Holliday?

A: Burt Lancaster played Wyatt and Kirk Douglas played Doc.

―――――?ὶ―――――

Q: Can you name the actor who played Wyatt in the 1967 movie, *Hour of the Gun*? Who played Doc?

A: James Garner played Wyatt. Jason Robards played Doc.

―――――?ὶ―――――

Q: Can you name the sheriff of Lincoln County, New Mexico, in 1881-1882?

A: Patrick Floyd Garrett (1850-1908).

―――――?ὶ―――――

Q: Can you name the sheriff of Dona Ana County, New Mexico, from 1896-1900?

A: Patrick Floyd Garrett (1850-1908). He was also appointed Deputy U.S. Marshal in 1896 and Collector of Customs at El Paso, Texas, in the early 1900s.

Q: Pat Garrett always said that he would die with his boots on. Did he?

A: Yes. He was shot from behind along a trail between Organ and Las Cruces, New Mexico, on February 29, 1908.

———————?———————

Q: Who assassinated Sheriff Pat Garrett?

A: Jesse Wayne Brazel confessed to shooting Garrett twice, once through the head and once through the back. He pled self-defense and was acquitted of murder when he was tried in April of the following year.

———————?———————

Q: How could Brazel claim self-defense when he shot Garrett twice from behind?

A: He claimed he was so afraid of the former sheriff because of his reputation as a gunman, that he was obliged to shoot him from behind. The jury bought it.

———————?———————

Q: Name the actors who played Sheriff Pat Garrett and Billy the Kid in the 1973 movie *Pat Garrett and Billy the Kid*.

A: James Coburn played Garrett. Kris Kristofferson played Billy.

———————?———————

Q: Name the two peace officers who were shot to death by Billy the Kid when he escaped from the Lincoln County Court House for the last time on April 28, 1881?

A: Robert Olinger (1841-1881), a sheriff's deputy in Dona Ana County, New Mexico, and James W. Bell (1853-1881), a Lincoln County deputy.

———————?———————

Q: Who played Billy the Kid in Arthur Penn's 1958 movie, *The Left-Handed Gun*?

A: Paul Newman. Billy the Kid was not left-handed. A reversed photographic plate used to produce the only picture of Billy known to exist made it appear that way. It made for a good movie title, anyway.

————————?¿————————

Q: Can you name the Army scout and Pinkerton detective who went wrong in the 1890s and was hanged for murder at Cheyenne, Wyoming, on November 20, 1903?

A: Tom Horn, who was born in Missouri in 1861. He served as an army scout for General Nelson Miles in the campaign against Geronimo and as a Pinkerton detective against train robbers before he became a hired gun for large Wyoming cattle interests.

————————?¿————————

Q: Who played Tom Horn in the 1980 movie of the same name?

A: Steve McQueen (1930-1980).

————————?¿————————

Q: In 1884, there was a gunfight in the village of Upper Frisco Plaza in western New Mexico in which a young Socorro County sheriff's deputy held off an attack by some eighty Texans for thirty-six hours. Can you name the deputy?

A: Elfego Baca (1865-1945). He later became Socorro County sheriff. He also later became an attorney and practiced law in Albuquerque for many years. Baca was a man who lived from the last year of the Civil War to the first year of the Atomic Age.

————————?¿————————

Q: What actor played the title roles in the 1962 movie, *Elfego Baca: Six Gun Law*, and the 1978 movie, *The Nine Lives of Elfego Baca*?

A: Robert Loggia (1930- --).

Q: This scout, marshal, gunfighter and gambler was shot to death in Deadwood, South Dakota, on August 2, 1876. What was his name?

A: Wild Bill Hickok (1837-1876).

Photo courtesy of the South Dakota State Historical Society

Q: What was Wild Bill Hickok's real name? Where was he from?

A: James Butler Hickok was born in LaSalle County, Illinois, in 1837.

Q: What position of authority did J. B. Hickok hold in Abilene, Kansas, in 1871?

A: He was town marshal. He spent most of his time, however, playing poker at the Alamo Saloon.

———————?¿———————

Q: Name the assassin who shot Wild Bill Hickok in the back of the head in Deadwood, South Dakota, on August 2, 1876, as the gunfighter sat playing poker in Saloon Number 10.

A: Jack McCall, a drifter and saddle tramp. He was ultimately hanged for the crime.

———————?¿———————

Q: What poker hand was Wild Bill holding when he was shot dead?

A: Legend is not clear on this point. Some stories say the hand was a full house, aces over eights. Others believe it was a full house, but eights over aces. Yet others say it was two pairs, aces and eights. Whichever it was, it has become known as the "dead man's hand." (If the latter was the case, the real question is, what was the fifth card?)

———————?¿———————

Q: Who played Wild Bill Hickok in the 1951-1956 television series of the same name? Who played his sidekick Jingles?

A: Guy Madison played Wild Bill. Andy Devine (1905-1977) played Jingles Jones.

———————?¿———————

Q: Can you name the Idaho lawman and scout who, for more than 40 years, from the early 1860s until after the turn of the century, served as deputy in Boise County, U.S. Marshal, and scout in the Nez Perce and Bannock Wars?

A: Orlando "Rube" Robbins (1836-1908).

Q: What organization, which operated throughout the Old West in the years following the Civil War (and is still with us today), was called "The Eye That Never Sleeps"?

A: The Pinkerton Detective Agency was formed as the Northwestern Police Agency in Chicago in 1855 by Allan Pinkerton (1819-1884). The agency had many successes in capturing Old West outlaws, but it never captured Butch Cassidy and the Sundance Kid.

———————?———————

Q: According to Lula Parker Betenson in *Butch Cassidy, My Brother*, who did the outlaw consider his best friend, the Sundance Kid or Elzy Lay?

A: Mrs. Betenson reported that Butch thought that Sundance drank too much and shot too quick. Elzy was "always dependable and levelheaded."

———————?———————

Q: Name the sheriff of Trinidad, Colorado, who was killed in a gunfight at Turkey Canyon, New Mexico, with outlaws Sam Ketchum, Harvey Logan (Kid Curry) and Elzy Lay (William McGinnis) in July of 1899.

A: Las Animas County Sheriff Edward Farr. A New Mexico posseman, H. N. Love, was also killed.

———————?———————

Q: What became of the outlaws after the gunfight at Turkey Canyon?

A: Sam Ketchum was wounded and later died. Elza Lay, one of Butch Cassidy's original Wild Bunch, was also wounded, captured, tried, convicted, and sentenced to life in prison. Kid Curry got clean away.

———————?———————

Q: How long was Elzy Lay's "life" prison sentence?

A: Elzy Lay, aka William McGinnis, entered the New Mexico territorial prison on October 10, 1899. He was pardoned by Gov. Miguel A. Otero in January of 1906. He gave up his life of crime after that.

———————?¿———————

Q: Name the Kansas and Texas gunfighter and gambler who became marshal of Austin, Texas, in 1880. His trademark was that he wore a high silk hat and carried a walking stick.

A: Ben Thompson (1843-1884). He admitted to having killed thirty-two men. He only served a year and a half as a lawman. His regular line of work was that of gambler. He was ambushed and killed, some said by hired killers, in San Antonio, along with Texas gunfighter King Fisher.

———————?¿———————

Q: Name the lawman who captured Oklahoma outlaw Bill Doolin as he soaked in a spa in Eureka Springs, Arkansas, in 1895.

A: Deputy U.S. Marshal Bill Tilghman who had previously served as town marshal in Dodge City, Kansas.

———————?¿———————

Q: Name the lawman who killed outlaw Bill Doolin near Lawson, Oklahoma, in the late summer of 1896.

A: Deputy U.S. Marshal Heck Thomas killed Doolin with a single shotgun blast as the outlaw, his wife and baby attempted to flee their hideout in the dark of the night.

———————?¿———————

Q: Deputy United States Marshals Bill Tilghman, Chris Madsen and Heck Thomas were known by what name in the Oklahoma Territory of the 1890s?

A: The Guardsmen.

———————?¿———————

Q: Who was the United States Marshal for the Oklahoma Territory who hired the Guardsmen?

A: U.S. Marshal Evett Nix. Under his direction, the Guardsmen put an end to the last remnants of the Dalton-Doolin gang and a lot of other banditry by the late 1890s.

———————?———————

Q: Gunfighter Dallas Stoudenmire (1843-1882) became the marshal of what Texas city in April of 1881?

A: El Paso. He served until the following year when he was shot to death in a gunfight in an El Paso saloon.

———————?———————

Q: In the early summer of 1884, Montana cattleman Granville H. Stuart (1835-1919) led a band of vigilantes against rustlers and horse thieves in eastern Montana. What did local folks call the group?

A: "Stuart's Stranglers." The stories vary, but it is believed they hung twenty to thirty miscreants. It is said that thievery dropped off considerably in eastern Montana in the years which followed.

———————?———————

Q: There was an active vigilante group in Socorro, New Mexico, in the 1880s. What was it called?

A: *Los colgadores*, which literally translates into English as "the hangers."

———————?———————

Q: Lynchings were the stock in trade of vigilantes in the Old West. Where did the expression "lynching," or "lynch law," come from?

A: It came from a self-appointed "judge" named William Lynch (1742-1820) who meted out capital punishment in Pennsylvania in the late 1700s.

Photo courtesy of the Utah State Historical Society

Q: This Utah lawman was known as "The Avenger," "The Executioner," "The Destroying Angel," and "Man of God, Son of Thunder." What was his name?

A: Orrin Porter "Port" Rockwell (1827-1878). The story goes that famed Mormon leader Joseph Smith told Rockwell to let his hair grow long and no enemy could harm him. None did, either.

Q: How many men died at the hands of Port Rockwell?

A: Sources report that he killed as many as a hundred men. That is not likely an accurate number, but he himself said he never killed anyone who didn't have it coming.

———————?¿———————

Q: How did Port Rockwell come to his end?

A: In June of 1878, he was found dead on a pile of hay in the Colorado Stables in Salt Lake City, Utah. There was speculation at the time that he had been poisoned. It is most likely he died of a heart attack.

———————?¿———————

Q: Who produced the first pistol with a revolving cylinder in the late 1830s?

A: Sam Colt (1814-1862) issued his first revolver in 1836. It was a .34 caliber five shooter with a short barrel (4").

———————?¿———————

Q: Why was the pistol carried by the Texas Rangers in the 1840s, and later by the U.S. Army, called the Walker Colt?

A: A Texas Ranger, Capt. Samuel Hamilton Walker (1817-1848), helped Colt modify his original gun into a bigger, heavier, larger caliber (.44 and .47) six-shooter, hence the Walker Colt.

———————?¿———————

Q: By what name was Texas Ranger William A. Wallace (1817-1899) better known?

A: Bigfoot. His exploits as a Ranger are legendary.

———————?¿———————

Q: In what year was the organization called the Texas Rangers created?

A: 1835. Originally they were a military force which guarded Texas borders and fought hostile Indians.

————?↲————

Q: There were Rangers in Texas and Rangers in Arizona. What was their New Mexico counterpart called?

A: The New Mexico Mounted Police existed from 1906 to 1921.

————?↲————

Q: What world heavyweight boxing champion, known as the Manassa Mauler or the Colorado Slugger, was born in the Old West?

A: William Harrison "Jack" Dempsey was born at Manassa, Colorado, in 1895. He was champion from 1919 when he defeated Jess Willard, to 1926 when he lost to Gene Tunney. He died in 1983.

————?↲————

OUTLAWS AND OTHER BLACK HAT GUYS

Some Were Worse Than Others

C H A P T E R 2

Q: Can you name the California stagecoach robber and doggerel poet who wrote this verse in 1877:

> I've labored long and hard for bread
> For honor and for riches
> But on my corns too long you've tread,
> You fine-haired sons-of-bitches.

A: Black Bart the Po 8 [*sic*]. His real name was probably Charles E. Bolton, but it may also have been C. E. Bolles. He was in his late 50s when he took up stage robbery in the late 1870s. He was captured in 1878 and sentenced to prison. He served a short term before being released.

———— ?¿ ————

Q: Name the sheriff of Beaverhead County, Montana, who was hanged by vigilantes for robbery and murder in 1864?

A: Henry Plummer (1835?-1864). He was leader of a gang which ranged widely over western Montana from Bannack to Virginia City. Some estimates are that there were as many as 200 men in his organization at various times, and that they killed more than 100 people.

Q: What did Henry Plummer's gang members call themselves?

A: "The Innocents." One source says that "I am innocent" was a code phrase gang members used to identify each other. It is also reported that they used secret handshakes and signals to communicate.

———————?¿———————

Q: What was unique about the way in which Henry Plummer was hanged?

A: The gallows was a tripod affair made of pine logs. As sheriff, Plummer had ordered it built. One source says he wanted to show the populace how he intended to deal with wrongdoers. Another says he intended to hang a political foe.

———————?¿———————

Q: What did the Bannack, Montana, vigilantes do after they dispatched outlaw gang leader Henry Plummer?

A: They set about settling old scores with other gang members. From early January to early February, 1864, they hanged twenty-four gang members.

———————?¿———————

Q: Speaking of executions, when early pioneers, traveling west by wagon train, were called upon to do a hanging on a treeless expanse of prairie, how would they improvise?

A: One solution was to change the method of execution from the rope to the firing squad. Another was to erect a makeshift gallows using wagon tongues, necessity being the mother of invention.

———————?¿———————

Q: Can you name the town marshal of Albuquerque, New Mexico, who was hanged for murder in February of 1883?

A: Milt Yarberry was Albuquerque's first town marshal. The name was probably an alias.

————————?⒰————————

Q: Who did Yarberry kill to get himself hanged?

A: In the spring of 1881, he killed a man who was his rival for the affections of a local widow. He was acquitted on a plea of self-defense. In June, he killed an innocent railroad worker who was just walking down the street. A plea of self-defense failed him that time.

————————?⒰————————

Q: What was unique about the way in which Milt Yarberry was hanged?

A: A special apparatus was used which employed a 400-pound counterweight which, when dropped, jerked the condemned man upwards. "Jerked to Jesus," as a local newspaper put it.

————————?⒰————————

Q: Oklahoma bank and train robber George Newcombe had a nickname. What was it?

A: "Bitter Creek." He and another outlaw, Charlie Pierce, were shot to death by Deputy U.S. Marshals near Guthrie, Oklahoma, in May of 1895.

————————?⒰————————

Q: Dave Mather was at various times a lawman and a convict. His dates of birth and death are not known, although he may have been born in 1844. He is known to have lived at various times in Denver, Colorado; Dodge City, Kansas; and Las Vegas, New Mexico. No one knew where he came from nor where he went when he disappeared in the late 1800s. What was his nickname?

A: Mysterious Dave.

Q: What bank and train robber was called the "King of Oklahoma Outlaws" by the middle of the 1890s?

A: Bill Doolin. Born in 1863, he was shot dead in the summer of 1896 by Deputy U.S. Marshal Heck Thomas. There were twenty-one shotgun pellets in his body.

———————?ι———————

Q: Tom Ketchum (1866-1901) was hanged for train robbery at Clayton, New Mexico in the spring of 1901. By what name was he better known?

A: Black Jack.

———————?ι———————

Q: What was unusual about the hanging of Tom Ketchum?

A: The execution was botched. The drop was too long and Ketchum's head was separated from his body.

———————?ι———————

Q: In the late 1890s, a gang of robbers made up of Bill Christian, his brother Bob, George Musgrave, and others, practiced thievery in Oklahoma, Texas, New Mexico, and Arizona. They were ambushed in 1897 near Clifton, Arizona, and Bill Christian is believed to have been killed. What did Bill Christian have in common with Tom Ketchum?

A: He also called himself "Black Jack."

———————?ι———————

Q: J. P. Miller (1863?-1909) was called "Killin' Jim" Miller. He is reported to have killed about twenty men in his lifetime. In February of 1909 he is alleged to have used a shotgun to kill Oklahoma lawman A. A. "Gus" Bobbitt. What then happened to Miller?

A: He and three other men were arrested for the crime and locked up at Ada, Oklahoma.

Q: Did the course of justice run true in the case of Killin' Jim Miller and his friends?

A: It depends on point of view. On April 19, 1909, a mob took them out of jail and to a nearby barn where each was hanged from a rafter one at a time.

———————?̷̣———————

Q: Why were Miller and his cohorts hanged one at a time?

A: The vigilantes only had one horse. They did have enough rope, though, to leave the bodies hanging until they could be photographed. The horse is in the picture, too.

———————?̷̣———————

Q: Name the outlaw gang which attempted to rob two banks at the same time in Coffeyville, Kansas, on October 5, 1892.

A: The Dalton Gang was made up of Bob, Emmett and Gratten Dalton, Bill Powers, and Dick Broadwell.

———————?̷̣———————

Q: Was the Dalton gang successful in robbing both banks?

A: No. When the shooting was over, all of the outlaws except Emmett Dalton were dead, and so were four townspeople.

———————?̷̣———————

Q: What became of twenty-one-year-old Emmett Dalton after this gunfight which claimed the lives of two of his brothers and two of his friends?

A: There were more than twenty bullet wounds in his body but he survived. He pled guilty to second-degree murder and was sentenced to life in prison. He was pardoned in 1907, married and moved to Los Angeles, California, where he became a respectable businessman. He died in 1937 of natural causes at the age of sixty-six.

Q: Dave Rudabaugh was a notorious killer, train and stagecoach robber and cattle thief in the 1870s and early 1880s from Arkansas to Arizona. With what New Mexico outlaw gang did he ride before being arrested and sentenced to hang?

A: He was with William Bonney, aka Billy the Kid, when the gang was captured at Stinking Springs, New Mexico, on Christmas Eve, 1880, by a posse led by Sheriff Pat Garrett.

————————?¿————————

Q: Did Dave Rudabaugh ever hang for any of the many crimes he committed?

A: Rudabaugh was sentenced to hang for the murder of Antonio Valdez, the jailer in Las Vegas, New Mexico. The execution was scheduled for April 22, 1881, but it was postponed while the case was appealed. Rudabaugh escaped from jail in December of 1881 and was never recaptured.

————————?¿————————

Q: Whatever became of Dave Rudabaugh?

A: It is generally believed that he spent a lot of time around the Arizona-Mexico border in the early 1880s. In late 1885 or early 1886, he is believed to have killed two Mexicans in a barroom fight in the city of Parral. He was then promptly killed by local folks, his head cut off and paraded around the town on the end of a stick. Mexican justice succeeded where the American version had failed.

————————?¿————————

Q: Jesse Wayne Brazel shot former sheriff Pat Garrett in the back and through the back of the head on February 29, 1908, and was acquitted of the murder the following year. What ever became of him?

A: He took up a homestead near Lordsburg, New Mexico, in the fall of 1909. In 1911 his wife died and the homestead was sold in 1913. In 1914 he disappeared from history. Even his son never knew for sure what happened to his father.

—————?¿—————

Q: What real life Old West character was played in the movies at various times by Johnny Mack Brown, Buster Crabbe, Dean White, Don Barry, Scott Brady, Tyler MacDuff, Roy Rogers, Jack Beutel, Lash LaRue, Nick Adams, Arthur Dexter, Audie Murphy, Paul Newman, Jack Taylor, Robert Taylor, Michael J. Pollard, Chuck Courtney, Kris Kristofferson, Emilio Estevez, Geoffrey Dueul, and others?

A: Billy the Kid (1859?-1881).

—————?¿—————

Q: What was Billy the Kid's real name?

A: The popular notion is that it was William Bonney (or Bony or Bonnie) but no one knows for sure. His mother's name was Antrim when she married Henry McCarty, and Billy called himself Kid Antrim at one time.

—————?¿—————

Q: One of the original members of Butch Cassidy's Wild Bunch was called Charley Jones, Camella Hanks or Deaf Charley. What was his real name?

A: O. C. "Charlie" Hanks was hard of hearing in one ear. Believed to have been a native of Las Vegas, New Mexico, where he committed his first murder, he also committed robberies and murders in Utah and Montana. He served nine years in the Montana state prison at Deer Lodge. He was released in 1901.

—————?¿—————

Q: How did Deaf Charlie come to the end of the trail?

A: He was killed by a policeman in a barroom gunfight in San Antonio, Texas, in 1902.

———?¿———

Q: What was Butch Cassidy's real name?

A: Robert Leroy Parker was born near Beaver, Utah, on April 13, 1866. According to his sister, his parents called him Leroy and his dozen brothers and sisters called him Bob.

———?¿———

Q: Where does the notion come from that his name was George Leroy Parker?

A: Charles Kelly in *The Outlaw Trail* says his name was George Leroy Parker. The 1880 census shows that Maximillian and Annie Parker had, as eldest son, one Robert L. Parker. That would tend to confirm the former. It is noted that the Pinkerton Agency's file listed the outlaw as both George Parker and George Cassidy.

———?¿———

Q: From whence did Bob Parker get the name Butch Cassidy?

A: First he became Roy Parker, then George Parker, then Ed Cassidy (presumably after Mike Cassidy, a cowboy he worked with as a youth), and then Butch Cassidy. He used many names in his criminal career.

———?¿———

Q: What was the Sundance Kid's real name?

A: Harry Alonzo Longbaugh was born in 1863. He acquired the nickname Sundance, which he hated, because as a teenager he was spent time in jail for horse theft at Sundance, in northeastern Wyoming.

———?¿———

Photo courtesy of the Utah State Historical Society

Q: Pictured here are some of the members of Butch Cassidy's Wild Bunch. Can you identify the five of them?

A: Left to right, standing, are Bill Carver and Harvey Logan. Seated are Harry Longbaugh (The Sundance Kid), Ben Kilpatrick and Robert Leroy Parker (Butch Cassidy). The picture was taken in Fort Worth, Texas, in 1900.

———————?¿———————

Q: Who played *Butch Cassidy and the Sundance Kid* in the 1969 movie?

A: Paul Newman and Robert Redford, respectively.

————————?¿————————

Q: When and where did Butch and Sundance bite the dust?

A: The Pinkerton Detective Agency closed out its file on the two outlaws by reporting them killed by soldiers in the village of San Vicente, Bolivia, in 1909.

————————?¿————————

Q: Who disputes that version of events?

A: Lula Parker Betenson, in *Butch Cassidy, My Brother*, says Butch returned to Circleville, Utah, in 1925 and that he died in an unnamed city in the Pacific Northwest in 1937.

————————?¿————————

Q: And the Sundance Kid?

A: Sundance was also reported to have returned to the U.S. and to have died and been buried under another name somewhere in New Mexico.

————————?¿————————

Q: George L. Curry was a big-time Wyoming cattle rustler who sometimes rode with Butch Cassidy's Wild Bunch. What was his nickname?

A: "Flat Nose" or "Big Nose" Curry. He was shot and killed by a Utah sheriff just after the turn of the century.

————————?¿————————

Q: What other Old West outlaw was known for his nose?

A: Big Nose George Parrott was a murderer and a stagecoach and train robber in the Dakota Territory. He was taken out of the jail at Rawlins, Wyoming, in 1881 and hanged from a telegraph pole.

————————?¿————————

Q: Harvey Logan was the most feared killer in Butch Cassidy's Wild Bunch. It is reported that he killed four men in street duels. What was his nickname?

A: Kid Curry. He committed suicide rather than face capture after a train robbery near Parachute, Colorado, in 1903.

———————?¿———————

Q: Who was "... the dirty little coward that shot Mr. Howard, [and] laid poor Jesse in his grave"?

A: Bob Ford. J. D. Howard was the alias Jesse James was using when Ford shot him in the back on April 3, 1882.

———————?¿———————

Q: Where did Jesse James die?

A: In the living room of his home in St. Joseph, Missouri. Jesse was thirty-four years old at the time.

———————?¿———————

Q: More than twenty actors played Jesse James in various movies over the years. Among them are Tyrone Power, Roy Rogers, Audie Murphy, Robert Wagner, and Robert Duvall. Who played Jesse in *The Long Riders* (1980)?

A: James Keach.

———————?¿———————

Q: What became of Bob Ford after he killed Jesse James and collected the reward?

A: In June of 1892 he was operating a saloon in Creede, Colorado. On the evening of the 24th, in revenge for the killing of Jesse James, Ed Kelly walked in and shot him to death with a shotgun.

———————?¿———————

Q: There were originally four Younger brothers who rode with the Jesse James gang. Can you name them?

A: John, Bob, Jim, and Cole.

————————?¿————————

Q: What ever became of the Younger boys?

A: John was killed by Pinkerton detectives in 1874. The other three were sentenced to life in prison after the Northfield, Minnesota, raid in 1876. Bob died in prison of tuberculosis in 1889. Jim committed suicide after being released from prison in 1901. Cole, also released from prison in 1901, went back to Missouri where he died of a heart attack in 1916.

————————?¿————————

Q: Who played Cole Younger in the 1980 movie, *The Long Riders*?

A: David Carradine.

————————?¿————————

Q: What became of Frank James after his brother, Jesse, was assassinated in April of 1882?

A: On October 5, 1882, at age thirty-nine, he surrendered to Missouri Governor Thomas T. Crittenden. He was tried for murder, acquitted and freed. He returned to the family farm and lived there until February of 1915 when he died of natural causes.

————————?¿————————

Q: Texas gunman John Wesley Hardin (1853-1895) is reported to have killed about forty men in his criminal career. What punishment did he receive for his "wild and reckless life"?

A: He was sentenced to twenty-five years in the Huntsville (Texas) prison in 1877 for the killing of a deputy sheriff named Charles Webb of Brown County. He served fifteen years. He was shot down the following year.

Q: Who killed John Wesley Hardin?

A: El Paso Constable John Selman shot Hardin in the back of the head on August 19, 1895, in the Acme Saloon in El Paso. Selman himself had been a hired gun during the Lincoln County War in New Mexico in the late 1870s.

———————?¿ ———————

Q: Name the killer and gunfighter who, while surveying the large crowd assembled at Giddings, Texas, in 1877, to see him hang, said, "I see a good many enemies around, and mighty few friends."

A: William P. "Bill" Longley was twenty-seven years old when he was hanged. He is believed to have killed thirty-two men in the years between 1865 and 1877, from Texas to South Dakota. His final words from the gallows were, "I deserve this fate. It is a debt I owe for a wild and reckless life. So long, everybody."

———————?¿ ———————

Q: Rowdy Joe Lowe was a saloon keeper, gambler, procurer, and gunfighter who operated establishments in Wichita and Newton, Kansas and Denver, Colorado between 1870 and 1880. What was his wife's name?

A: Katherine, or Rowdy Kate. She operated Joe's brothels. Most of Joe's gunfights were over Kate, and he was finally shot to death in Denver in 1880.

———————?¿ ———————

Q: At what maximum range were the handguns of the Old West effective?

A: Anyone who could consistently hit a man, or a man-sized target, at fifty feet was considered very proficient with a Colt .45 caliber single-action revolver.

———————?¿ ———————

Q: Why was the first shot so important in a gunfight or gun duel in the Old West before 1895?

A: Because so much smoke was produced by the first shot that it was unlikely a shooter would be able to see the target for a second shot. So-called smokeless gunpowder came into use by about 1895.

———————?ι ———————

Q: The Colt Navy revolver, manufactured from 1851 to 1873, was also popular among many guntoters in the Old West. What caliber was it?

A: It was a .36 caliber. Wild Bill Hickok carried two of them in his sash, butts forward.

———————?ι ———————

Q: What was a "plow handle" in the jargon of the Old West?

A: A gun butt or pistol grip.

———————?ι ———————

Q: Jesse James carried a Smith and Wesson .45 caliber, single-action revolver. With what kind of a gun was he killed?

A: A Smith and Wesson .45 caliber, single-action revolver.

———————?ι ———————

Q: The forerunners of the modern-day "Saturday Night Specials" were available in .22 to .31 calibers for $2.00 to $5.00 in the Old West. What were such guns called back then?

A: Suicide specials.

———————?ι ———————

Q: The Colt Peacemaker, a .45 caliber, single-action revolver, with a seven and one-half-inch barrel and wood grips was introduced in 1873. How much did a Peacemaker cost by mail order?

A: $17.00. Remington pistols sold for $7.00 to $12.00, depending on the caliber and model. A similar Smith and Wesson pistol cost $13.00 to $14.00.

―――――?―――――

Q: What was the smallest caliber considered effective by the gunmen of the Old West?

A: The .32. Cole Younger, one of the Jesse James Gang, carried a Smith and Wesson .32 single-action.

―――――?―――――

Q: What is generally considered to have been the first practical lever-action rifle? It was first issued in 1860.

A: The Henry .44 caliber.

―――――?―――――

Q: What was the difference between a Winchester .44 carbine and a Winchester .44 rifle?

A: The rifle barrel was four inches longer than that of the carbine.

―――――?―――――

Q: In the Old West, what was considered the most fearsome weapon of all, especially at close range?

A: The ten or twelve gauge double-barrel shotgun with the barrels sawed off to eighteen or twenty inches. Doc Holliday carried one in the Gunfight at the O.K. Corral in 1881 and Deputy U.S. Marshal Heck Thomas used one to kill outlaw Bill Doolin in 1896.

―――――?―――――

Q: In the total history of western outlawry, Oklahoma brothers Al, Frank, Ed and John were probably the most unsuccessful train robbers of all in the 1880s. What was their last name?

A: Jennings. Al (1863-1961) and his brothers completely failed to stop several trains before they robbed one which was stopped to take on water. They got $60.00. Within a couple of days, Al, Frank and John were in custody and Ed was shot dead. Al and Frank were sentenced to prison and that was the end of the Jennings Gang.

———————?ₑ———————

Q: Who played the title role in the 1951 movie *Al Jennings of Oklahoma*, a highly fictionalized version of the would-be robber's life?

A: Dan Duryea (1907-1968).

———————?ₑ———————

Q: Can you name the beloved Texas badman who, along with five others, robbed the Union Pacific train of $60,000 near Big Springs, Nebraska, on August 18 (or September 19), 1877, and got away with it?

A: Sam Bass (1851-1878). The thieves got 3,000 freshly minted twenty dollar gold pieces. It was considered the largest train robbery in history up to that time.

———————?ₑ———————

Q: What became of young Sam Bass after the Big Springs robbery?

A: He died July 21, 1878 of a bullet wound in the stomach. This wound was received at the hands of Texas Ranger George Harrell in the town of Round Rock, Texas, while Sam was planning the robbery of the local bank.

———————?ₑ———————

Q: Can you name the Texas stagecoach robber who always made sure he left each passenger at least one dollar for breakfast?

A: Sam Bass.

Photo courtesy of the Denver Public Library, Western History Department

Q: This man was instrumental in the capture of Geronimo in Arizona in the 1880s, chased train and bank robbers in Colorado for Pinkerton's in the 1890s and was hanged for murder in Wyoming in 1903. Can you name him?

A: Born in Missouri in 1861, Tom Horn was hanged on November 20, 1903, at Cheyenne for the murder of a fourteen-year-old boy, the son of a sheepherder, who was shot from ambush.

Q: Ned Christie was an Oklahoma bootlegger, horse thief, bandit, and killer who was tracked down by Deputy U.S. Marshal Heck Thomas and a sixteen-man posse in 1892. (A second source says the posse was led by Deputy Marshal Paden Tolbert.) What made it difficult to capture Christie?

A: Christie had built himself a fort-like structure near Tahlequah. It took a cannon, dynamite, and a reported 2,000 rounds of sidearm fire to dislodge him. Christie was finally killed as he fled the structure.

————?ɩ ————

Q: It has been said the only man Billy the Kid feared was a diminutive killer by the name of Jesse Evans. What became of Evans after he left the Lincoln County War in 1879?

A: He fled to Texas where he killed a Ranger named Red Bingham in July of 1880. Sentenced to ten years in prison, he escaped from Huntsville in May of 1882 and disappeared from history. He was never recaptured.

————?ɩ ————

Q: Who played Jesse Evans in the 1970 movie *Chisum*?
A: Richard Jaeckel.

————?ɩ ————

Q: Name the New Mexico outlaw called the Sandia Mounta Desperado, who operated in the mountains north and east Albuquerque in the 1880s.

A: Marino Leyba. He was killed by Santa Fe County sheriff's deputies near Golden (New Mexico) in 1886.

————?ɩ ————

Q: What Texas/New Mexico gunman and killer called himself a "shootist"?

A: Clay Allison (1841-1887).

——————?¿——————

Q: Upon what tombstone will you find the inscription,
　　　HE NEVER KILLED A MAN
　　　THAT DID NOT NEED KILLING

A: The one that marks the grave of Clay Allison in Pecos, Texas. The statement is wide of the mark. Allison was involved in several questionable killings.

——————?¿——————

Q: How did gunman/gunfighter Clay Allison die?

A: On July 1, 1877, he fell off a freight wagon which ran over him, crushing him to death.

——————?¿——————

Q: Name the California gold robber and horse thief who may, or may not, have been killed and beheaded by a Texas Ranger named Harry Love in 1853.

A: Joaquin Murietta (1830?-1853?). In June of 1853, Harry Love displayed a large glass jar containing a human head which he claimed was that of Murietta. Whether it really was or not has been in dispute from that day to this.

——————?¿——————

Q: Cranford, or Crawford, Goldsby was a notorious killer in the Indian Territory. When asked if he had anything to say before he was hanged in 1896, he said, "I came here to die, not make a speech." By what name was he better known?

A: Cherokee Bill. He was twenty years old when he was hanged, sentenced to death by Judge Isaac Parker at Fort Smith, Arkansas. Goldsby had killed thirteen men.

——————?¿——————

39

Q: Name the Mormon Bishop who was responsible for the so-called Mountain Meadows massacre in southwestern Utah in September 1857, in which 120 men, women and children were killed by Indians and Mormons.

A: John D. Lee. The atrocity was covered up for many years, but in 1875, Lee was accused of the crime. He was tried and ultimately convicted. He was executed by firing squad at Salt Lake City in March of 1877.

————?¿————

Q: Who was the Oklahoma/Arkansas outlaw believed to have been the first to use an automobile in the commission of a bank robbery?

A: Henry Starr (1881-1921), said to have been Belle Starr's nephew. He began using a car in his robberies in 1914. In 1921 his car broke down after a robbery at Harrison, Arkansas, and he was killed in a gunfight with sheriff's deputies. They had pursued him with their own cars. Starr is believed to have robbed nearly fifty banks in his career.

————?¿————

Q: Joseph Alfred "Captain Jack" Slade (1824-1864) was shot five times at close range by one Jules Reni at Julesburg, Colorado, in 1858, but survived. What did Jack Slade do to Jules Reni a year or so later?

A: Some of Slade's friends caught Reni and tied him to a corral post at Slade's ranch near Cold Springs, Colorado, where he remained overnight. Next morning, Slade used the hapless Reni for target practice, swilling whiskey between shots. Reni died with more than twenty bullet holes in him. According to legend, Slade then cut off one of his ears and used it for a watch fob.

————?¿————

Q: How did Jack Slade meet his end?

A: After getting drunk and shooting up the town, he was hanged for disorderly conduct at Virginia City, Montana, in March of 1864.

———————?¿———————

Q: How were Jack Slade's remains disposed of?

A: His wife put his body in an alcohol-filled metal casket with intentions of returning the body to Illinois for burial. She got as far as Salt Lake City. Jack's sodden remains were buried there in July, 1864.

———————?¿———————

Q: Jefferson Randolph Smith (1860-1898) was a saloon keeper, con man, thief and killer who migrated from Creede, Colorado, to Skagway, Alaska, in 1897. What was his nickname?

A: Soapy.

———————?¿———————

Q: Why was Jefferson Randolph Smith known as Soapy?

A: One of his early scams involved selling bars of soap for $5.00 on the premise that among his inventory were some bars which were wrapped in $20 and $50 bills.

———————?¿———————

Q: What ever became of Soapy Smith?

A: His scams and thievery were so outrageous that the good people of Skagway, Alaska, became aroused. When some of Soapy's henchmen stole nearly $3,000 from a prospector named John Stewart in July of 1898, local folks met as vigilantes to consider the matter. Soapy tried to crash the meeting and a man by the name of Frank Reid shot him dead. Smith managed to shoot Reid who lived for nearly two weeks before he, too, died.

Q: Name the Old West gambler and gunfighter whose physical stature was completely consistent with his name.

A: Luke Short (1854-1893). He was described as diminutive by one source and small in stature by another. He was also described as deadly with a pistol. The first man he killed was a luckless drunk and itinerant gunfighter named Charlie Storms, in Tombstone, Arizona Territory, February 1881.

———————?ι ———————

Q: Name the former New Mexico lawman who eventually ended up in Fort Worth, Texas, where he set up a detective agency, the primary purpose of which was to shake down local gamblers. He also had a minor reputation as a gunfighter.

A: Jim Courtright (1848-1887). A native of Iowa, he served as town marshal in Lake Valley, New Mexico. He died with his boots on in Texas.

———————?ι ———————

Q: Who were the well-known participants in a street gunfight in Fort Worth, Texas, in February 1887?

A: Luke Short and Jim Courtright. Luke Short won.

———————?ι ———————

Q: Luke Short lived by the gun. Did he die by the gun?

A: No. He died of dropsy in Kansas in 1893.

———————?ι ———————

EXPLORERS, SOLDIERS AND SCOUTS

Buckskins, Blue Coats & Gray

CHAPTER 3

Q: Can you name the two soldiers who led the twenty-eight-month scouting expedition from St. Louis to the Pacific Ocean beginning May 14, 1804?

A: Mariwether Lewis (1774-1809), previously an infantry captain, and William Clark (1770-1838), an artillery lieutenant.

————?—————

Q: Was the westward march of Lewis and Clark an aggressive military expedition?

A: No. President Thomas Jefferson (1743-1826) had received assurances from the governments of Spain, England and France that they would not interfere with Lewis and Clark.

————?—————

Q: At age fourteen, in 1824, famed scout Kit Carson was "bound" to tradesman David Workman in Franklin, Missouri, to learn saddle-making. He ran away to the West in 1826. What reward was offered for his return?

A: According to a newspaper notice dated October 6, 1926, the reward offered was one cent ($0.01).

————————?¿————————

Q: The army officer pictured below, along with more than 200 other officers and enlisted men, was killed in the Battle of the Little Bighorn River, Montana, in June of 1876. Can you name him?

A: George Armstrong Custer (1839-1876) as he appeared at age seventeen when he began his military career as a cadet at West Point, class of 1861.

Photo courtesy of the Wyoming State Museum

Photo courtesy of Wyoming State Museum

Q: This horse was the only U.S. Army survivor of the Battle of the Little Bighorn, June 25, 1876. Was it in fact General Custer's favorite mount, the gelding called Vic?

A: No. This cavalry horse was named Comanche. Gen. George Armstrong Custer and five troops of the Seventh U.S. Cavalry were wiped out to a man by a superior force of Sioux and Cheyenne Indians.

———————?¿———————

Q: Comanche belonged to which of Custer's officers?

A: Capt. Miles W. Keogh, commanding officer of I Company. The horse had seven bullet wounds but recovered and was retired and never ridden again. Comanche died in 1891, fifteen years after his master was killed.

Q: The name of the Custer Battlefield National Monument was changed to what in 1992?

A: President George Bush signed legislation which changed the name to Little Bighorn Battlefield National Monument.

———?¿———

Q: Who was instrumental in bringing about the name change?

A: The bill to change the name was introduced by Congressman Ben Nighthorse Campbell of Colorado, the only American Indian serving in the U.S. Congress.

———?¿———

Q: Who played General Custer in the movie, *Little Big Man*?
A: Richard Mulligan.

———?¿———

Q: Who played General Custer in the 1941 movie, *They Died with Their Boots On*?

A: Errol Flynn (1909-1959).

———?¿———

Q: Who was in command of the U.S Army troops who attacked the Cheyenne Indian camp on the Washita River on the morning of November 27, 1868?

A: Lt. Col. (Bvt. Maj. Gen.) George Armstrong Custer.

———?¿———

Q: General Custer had the Seventh Cavalry band accompany him into the field on the winter march which led up to the attack on the Indian camps on the Washita River, in November 1868. What musical piece did the band play as the troops shot Indians?

A: An Irish drinking song called *Garryowen*.

Q: Capt. Frederick William Benteen (1834-1898) joined the Seventh Cavalry when it was formed in 1866. He served with Custer until the general's death at the Little Bighorn in 1876. What was Benteen's opinion of Custer?

A: Benteen wrote a narrative of the events leading up to the massacre and he carried on a wide correspondence between 1876 and his death in 1898. Of Custer he said, "I am only too proud to say that I despised him."

———————?⸻———————

Q: "Grant's Peace Policy" was developed early in the presidential administration (1869-1877) of Ulysses S. Grant (1822-1885). What event doomed it to failure?

A: On January 23, 1870, Maj. Eugene Baker and two troops of the Second Cavalry attacked a Piegen Indian camp on the Marias River in Montana. The troops killed 120 men and 53 women and children.

———————?⸻———————

Q: Name the U.S. Army officer who was appointed commander of New Mexico's Fort Union in 1876, court-martialed in 1877, reassigned as commander of Fort Stanton in 1878 and court-martialed again in 1879.

A: Lt. Col. Nathan A. M. Dudley. It was he who ordered U.S. Army troops into the town of Lincoln in 1878 during the so-called Five Day Battle of the Lincoln County War. He survived in the Army because of political connections. He died in 1910 with the rank of Brigadier General.

———————?⸻———————

Q: What U.S. Army officer was arguably the greatest of them all as an Indian fighter having fought in the Red River War (1874-1875), the Sioux Wars (1876-1881), the Nez Perce Retreat (1877), the campaign against Geronimo (1886) and at Wounded Knee (1890-1891)?

A: Gen. Nelson A. Miles (1839-1925).

―――――?―――――

Q: What U.S. military commander in Texas during the 1870s was called "Pecos Bill"?

A: Lt. Col. William Rufus Shafter (1835-1906) of the Twenty-fourth Infantry. He was also a troop commander during the Spanish American War in Cuba in 1898.

―――――?―――――

Q: Who was the commander of the First New Mexico Volunteer Infantry which waged a brutal war of conquest against the Navajos in 1863-1864?

A: Col. Christopher "Kit" Carson (1809-1868). It was an assignment he did not much like. He said, "I can take no pride in this fearful destruction. My sleep is haunted by dreams of starving Navajo squaws and children."

―――――?―――――

Q: The first settlers reached Oregon over the Rocky Mountains in November of 1841. Name the scout who showed them the way.

A: An Irishman named Thomas "Broken Hand" Fitzpatrick (1799-1854). He was called Broken Hand because of an accidental injury to his wrist.

―――――?―――――

Q: Name the scout and Indian agent who served as go-between when Gen. Oliver Howard met with the Apache Chief Cochise in 1872, and who helped keep peace with the Apache until 1876.

A: A New Yorker by the name of Tom Jeffords (1832-1914).

―――――?―――――

Q: Who played Cochise in the 1950 movie, *Broken Arrow?*

A: Jeff Chandler (1918-1961). John Hodiak (1914-1955) played Cochise in the 1953 movie, *Conquest of Cochise*.

—————?ₑ—————

Q: Can you name this famed U.S. Army scout and hunter pictured below?

A: William Frederick Cody (1846-1917).

—————?ₑ—————

Photo courtesy of the Wyoming State Museum

Q: How did Bill Cody come to be called Buffalo Bill?

A: By his own account he killed 4,200 buffalo, in eight months, to feed a railroad crew laying track near Hays City, Kansas, in 1867.

—————?ₑ—————

Q: What was unique about the Ninth and Tenth Cavalry Regiments and the Twenty-fourth and Twenty-fifth Infantry Regiments, all of which fought extensively in the Indian Wars following the Civil War?

A: These regiments were made up entirely of black troopers except for the officers who were all white.

———————?———————

Q: What were black soldiers, fighting on the western frontier during the last half of the nineteenth century, called by their Indian foes?

A: They were called Buffalo Soldiers. The origin of the name is uncertain although some believe the Indians saw a similarity between the hair of the black soldier and that of the buffalo. The troopers accepted the name proudly. A buffalo was featured on their regimental emblem.

———————?———————

Q: Who was the most famous military leader to command the Tenth Cavalry in combat against Indians in Montana and Pancho Villa in Old Mexico?

A: Gen. John J. "Black Jack" Pershing (1860-1948) was with the Tenth for ten years.

———————?———————

Q: What was General Pershing's assessment of his black troops?

———————?———————

A: He said this in 1921:
> It has been an honor which I am proud to claim to have been at one time a member of that intrepid organization of the Army which has always added glory to the military history of America -- the Tenth Cavalry.

50

Q: Name the first black officer assigned to the U.S. Army's Tenth Cavalry Regiment. (A clue: he was also the first black man to graduate from West Point.)

A: Lt. Henry O. Flipper graduated from West Point in 1877. He was assigned to the Tenth Cavalry and posted to Fort Concho, and later to Fort Davis, both in Texas.

————?——————

Q: What was the unfortunate end to Lieutenant Flipper's military career?

A: He was court-martialed in 1881 on what many considered, then and now, as trumped-up charges. Acquitted of an embezzlement charge but convicted of "conduct unbecoming an officer," he was dismissed from the service. Many believed that white officers, including Lt. Col. William "Pecos Bill" Shafter, conspired against Flipper because he was observed horseback riding with a white woman.

————?——————

Q: Who was the commander of the Texas Confederates who invaded New Mexico during the Civil War and advanced to Glorieta Pass, east of Santa Fe, before being turned back by Union volunteers from New Mexico and Colorado?

A: Gen. Henry Hopkins Sibley (1816-1886) led the 1862 invasion. He had previously served as an officer in the United States Army at Fort Union, New Mexico Territory.

————?——————

Q: Who was in command of the flanking movement of the Union's New Mexico and Colorado Volunteers which defeated Confederate troops under Gen. H. H. Sibley at the Glorieta Pass in 1862?

A: Maj. John M. Chivington (1821-1894).

51

Q: Who was in command of a troop of Colorado Volunteers in 1864 when they attacked a village of Cheyenne and Arapaho Indians at Sand Creek and killed more than 300 men, women and children?

A: Col. John M. Chivington (1821-1894). He is quoted as having said, "I am fully satisfied that to kill the red rebels is the only way to have peace and quiet."

————?¿————

Q: What was John M. Chivington's occupation before he took up a career as a military man?

A: He was a Methodist minister. He turned down an opportunity to serve as a chaplain to become a fighting soldier.

————?¿————

Q: Who was the commanding officer of the so-called "Army of the West" which captured Santa Fe, New Mexico, for the United States during the Mexican War without firing a single shot in August of 1846?

A: Gen. Stephen Watts Kearny (1794-1848).

————?¿————

Q: How did General Kearny propose to govern the newly-acquired *Nuevo Mejico*, which then included all of what is now Arizona and parts of Colorado, Utah and Nevada?

A: He established what came to be called the Kearny Code, based on both American and Mexican law. He also appointed a civil government.

————?¿————

Photo courtesy of the Denver Public Library, Western History Department

Q: What frontier army officer, pictured above, said in 1866, "Give me eighty men and I would ride through the whole Sioux Nation"?

A: Capt. (Bvt. Lt. Col.) William J. Fetterman.

———————?¿———————

Q: Did Captain Fetterman ever get a chance to ride through the Sioux Nation?

A: On December 21, 1866, Fetterman was in command of seventy-eight soldiers, and two civilians, when they rode out of Fort Phil Kearney, Dakota Territory, in pursuit of a Sioux raiding party. They encountered an estimated 2,000 Indians at Peno Creek, only a short distance from the fort. Fetterman's command was wiped out to a man.

———————?¿————————

Q: What famed general and veteran of the Civil War so hated the American Southwest he suggested that the United States go back to war to force Mexico to take New Mexico and Arizona back?

A: William Tecumseh Sherman (1820-1891).

———————?¿————————

Q: What was the name of the young U.S. Army Lieutenant and explorer who was among the very first Americans to enter the Spanish-ruled Southwest in 1806-1807?

A: Zebulon Montgomery Pike (1779-1813). He and his small band were captured by Spanish troops in southern Colorado in early 1807. They were taken first to Santa Fe and then on to Chihuahua before being released.

———————?¿————————

Q: What unconventional U.S. Army general waged war against the Piutes, Sioux and Apache and later joined the Indian Rights Association?

A: Gen. George Crook (1828-1890). He was described by one contemporary writer as ". . . a wise, large-hearted, large-minded, strong-handed, broad-gauge man. . . ."

———————?¿————————

Q: Can you name the only U.S. Army general officer to be killed by Indians during the Indian Wars of the latter half of the nineteenth century?

A: Unarmed, Brig. Gen. Edward R. S. Canby was shot full in the face and died instantly on April 11, (Good Friday) 1873, during a peace conference with Modoc Indians in the Lava Beds near the California/Oregon border.

————?——————

Q: Who killed General Canby?

A: The Modoc Indian Chief Kintpuash (or Kientpoos), also known as Captain Jack. He was captured on June 3, tried, and hanged for murder on October 3, 1873.

————?——————

Q: Who was in command of fifty "first-class hardy frontiersmen" who were set upon by 600 to 700 (some sources say 1,000) Sioux and Cheyenne Indians at Beecher's Island, in the Arikaree Fork of the Republican River in Colorado, September 17, 1868?

A: Maj. George A. Forsyth. He and his charges, military and civilian, held out for more than a week until a relief column of Buffalo Soldiers from the Tenth Cavalry under Capt. Louis H. Carpenter arrived. Forsyth reported six of his command and thirty-five Indians killed.

————?——————

Q: During the latter nineteenth century, the U.S. Army's Military Division of the Missouri extended from Fort Brown in far south Texas to Fort Benton in northern Montana and Fort Cameron in western Utah. Where was it headquartered?

A: Chicago, Illinois.

————?——————

Q: Who succeeded Gen. William Tecumseh Sherman as commandant of the Military Division of Missouri in 1869 and held the position for fourteen years?

A: Gen. Philip Henry Sheridan (1831-1888) who had previously been second in command.

————?¿————

Q: What were Gen. Phil Sheridan's orders to General Custer when he sent the Seventh Cavalry against the Indian Chief Black Kettle at the Washita River in 1868?

A: "Kill or hang all warriors and bring back all women and children."

————?¿————

Q: Did Gen. Phil Sheridan really say, "The only good Indian is a dead Indian"?

A: Not exactly. What he really said was, "The only good Indians I ever saw were dead."

————?¿————

Q: Who was the U.S. Army officer in command of troops which defeated the Santee Sioux at Wood Lake, Minnesota, on September 23, 1862, following the so-called Minnesota Massacre of the preceding August?

A: Col. Henry Hastings Sibley, not to be confused with the Confederate General Henry Hopkins Sibley who led the Texas invasion of New Mexico in the spring of 1862.

————?¿————

Q: Who was in command at the Alamo, near San Antonio, Texas, on Sunday, March 6, 1836, when the fortress was taken by 4,000 Mexican troops under Gen. Antonio Lopez de Santa Anna?

A: Lt. Col. William Barret Travis (1809-1836) was in command of the 183 defenders.

————?¿————

Q: Name two other well-known frontiersmen who died that day in south Texas.

A: Jim Bowie (1799-1836) of Louisiana and Davy Crockett (1786-1836) of Tennessee.

———————?¿———————

Q: Can you name the actors cast in the roles of Travis, Bowie, and Crockett in the epic 1960 movie, *The Alamo*?

A: Laurence Harvey (1928-1973) played Travis, Richard Widmark played Bowie and John Wayne (1907-1979) played Crockett.

———————?¿———————

Q: All of the 183 defenders of the Alamo were killed by Mexican Army troops. How many Mexican troops were killed in the battle?

A: Some estimates range as high as 1,500, about eight Mexicans for each Texan. It is not possible to be specific because General Santa Anna ordered the bodies of his dead troops burned. Bodies of the Alamo's defenders were also burned.

———————?¿———————

Q: What second military misfortune befell the Texans seeking independence from Mexico on March 19, 1836?

A: Col. James Fannin and about 400 Texans were overwhelmed and captured by a force of 1,400 Mexican troops under Gen. Jose Urrea a few miles from Goliad in south Texas.

———————?¿———————

Q: What became of Colonel Fannin?

A: On Palm Sunday, March 27, 1836, Mexican troops conducted mass executions of the prisoners captured at Goliad. Only about sixty of them survived. Colonel Fanin (1804-1836) was among those executed.

———————?¿———————

Q: Where did Sam Houston and Texas get revenge on General Santa Anna for the massacres at the Alamo and Goliad?

A: On April 21, 1836, a force of about 800 Texans under Houston's command attacked a force of more than 1,200 Mexicans near the San Jacinto River in east Texas.

———————?¿———————

Q: What was the outcome of the Battle of San Jacinto, Texas, April 21, 1836?

A: About half the Mexicans troops were killed and the remainder, including General Santa Anna, were captured. Only six Texans died in the attack. The Battle of San Jacinto secured Texas independence from Mexico.

———————?¿———————

Q: What became of the Mexican dictator, Gen. Antonio Lopez de Santa Anna (1795-1876) after his defeat at San Jacinto?

A: Sam Houston spared his life. He was held prisoner in Texas until November 1836, and then allowed to return to Mexico.

———————?¿———————

Q: Name the Confederate guerrilla leader who led about 450 mounted irregulars during the Civil War in the sacking of Lawrence, in eastern Kansas, on August 21, 1863?

A: William Clarke Quantrill (1837-1865). About 150 of the town's residents were killed and the town was burned.

———————?¿———————

Q: Is it correct to say that Frank and Jesse James were among Quantrill's guerrillas at the raid on Lawrence?

A: At age twenty, Frank was probably there. At age sixteen, Jesse probably was not.

Q: With what Confederate guerrilla leader did both Frank and Jesse ride?

A: Bill Anderson, better known as "Bloody Bill." He was killed in October 1864, before the Civil War ended.

———————?₂———————

Q: What raid did Bloody Bill Anderson lead which gave him and the James Brothers a place in the history book of dishonor?

A: The raid on Centralia, Missouri, September 27, 1864. About 225 guerrillas plundered the town, then robbed a train and murdered more than twenty Union soldiers who were only there as passengers. They then slaughtered a contingent of Union troops which pursued them.

———————?₂———————

Q: When and where was the last armed invasion of the United States by foreign troops?

A: On March 9, 1916, Columbus, New Mexico, was attacked by troops under the command of Mexican revolutionary leader Pancho Villa. There has been debate from that day to this as to whether Villa personally participated in the raid.

———————?₂———————

Q: Who suffered the most casualties in the raid on Columbus, New Mexico, in March of 1916 -- Mexicans or Americans?

A: About one hundred Villistas were killed along with sixteen Americans, soldiers and civilians alike.

———————?₂———————

Q: What U.S. Army General commanded a "punitive foray" against Pancho Villa after the Columbus raid?

A: Gen. John J. "Black Jack" Pershing (1860-1948). By June of 1916, President Woodrow Wilson had ordered 100,000 troops to the Mexican border. Pershing never caught Villa.

————¿?————

THE INDIANS OF THE WEST AND THEIR CHIEFS

From Apache to Zuni

CHAPTER 4

Q: What was the fate of the Mimbres Apache leader Mangas Coloradas (1795-1863)?

A: He surrendered to the U.S. Army in January 1863. Shortly thereafter, he was tied down by a group of soldiers who burned him with hot bayonets before they shot him to death.

———————?¿———————

Q: What was the "official" description of Mangas Coloradas' death?

A: He was shot while attempting escape. No explanation was given regarding the fact that he was scalped and mutilated.

———————?¿———————

Q: To what band of Apaches did Geronimo (1829-1909) belong?

A: Chiricahua (pronounced Cheer-ah-cow-ah).

———————?¿———————

Q: What was Geronimo's real name?

A: Three different sources give it three different spellings: Gokhlayeh, Goyathlay and Goyalka. One source says it translates as "the yawner."

———————?¿———————

Q: In March of 1886, after almost a year on the warpath, Geronimo met with Gen. George Crook in northern Mexico and agreed to surrender. How is it, then, that the U.S. war with the Apache continued until September 1886?

A: Once agreement was reached, General Crook and his main body of troops departed for Fort Apache leaving behind a small detachment to escort the Indians north. Unfortunately, a merchant showed up with a wagon load of whisky. Geronimo and his followers began to drink and retreated back into the mountains of northern Mexico.

———————?¿———————

Q: Geronimo and the remaining thirty-seven of his followers (fourteen of whom were women and children) finally surrendered to what United States Army General in September of 1886?

A: Gen. Nelson Appleton Miles (1839-1925). The surrender took place at Skeleton Canyon near the New Mexico/Arizona line.

———————?¿———————

Q: What became of Geronimo after he surrendered to the U.S. Army in 1886?

A: He was imprisoned in Florida until 1894 when he was moved to Fort Sill, Oklahoma.

———————?¿———————

Q: How did he live out the rest of his days?

A: He appeared in President Theodore Roosevelt's inaugural parade in 1901 and at the World's Fair in St. Louis in 1904. He earned a meager living by making and selling Indian artifacts and pictures of himself. Geronimo was never allowed to return to the desert Southwest. He died at Fort Sill in 1909.

———————?¿———————

Q: Is it accurate to say that the Apache always scalped their slain enemies?

A: No, it isn't. The Apache rarely scalped their victims. Their raids were conducted for plunder and for those items not provided by nature (weapons, horses, even money). There was no status among the Apache attached to keeping accounts on the number of enemies killed by any given warrior.

———————?¿———————

Q: Is it accurate to say that the Apache in general, and Geronimo in particular, were among the very best guerrilla fighters on the western frontier?

A: Yes, it is. Here is what Lt. Britton Davis said about Geronimo's band:

> In this campaign, thirty-five men and eight half-grown or older boys, encumbered with the care and sustenance of 101 women and children, with no base of supplies and no means of waging war or obtaining food or transportation other than what they could take from their enemies, maintained themselves for eighteen months in a country two hundred by four hundred miles in extent, against 5,000 troops, regulars and irregulars, five hundred Indian auxiliaries of these troops, and an unknown number of civilians.

Q: What was the name of the San Juan Pueblo Indian medicine man who, while in hiding at Taos Pueblo, New Mexico, organized the Pueblo Indian Revolt of 1680?

A: Popé (?-1690).

———————?&———————

Q: Who was the Sauk and Fox Indian from Oklahoma who won gold medals in both the pentathlon and decathlon at the Stockholm Olympics in 1912?

A: Jim Thorpe (1886-1953). He won the medals only to have them taken away when it was learned that he had previously been paid to play baseball.

———————?&———————

Q: Who starred in the 1951 movie, *Jim Thorpe -- All American*?

A: Burt Lancaster.

———————?&———————

Q: What educational institution opened in 1879 with the avowed aim to " . . . kill the Indian and save the man."

A: The Carlisle Indian School at Carlisle, Pennsylvania, was founded by Richard Henry Pratt, a former army officer, scout and Indian fighter. It was the prototype for a network of Indian boarding schools which aimed at Indian acculturation.

———————?&———————

Q: Pawnee Indians under Sky Chief and Crow Indians under Chief Plenty Coups provided the U.S. Army with scouts in the 1870s. Why did they do so?

A: Both chiefs believed that the Army would ultimately win the Indian Wars and they wanted to be in a favorable position with military authorities.

———————?&———————

Photo courtesy of the Denver Public Library, Western History Department

Q: Partial to white men's ways, this Colorado Ute Indian chief aligned himself with U.S. Secretary of the Interior Carl Shurz in concluding the Ute Indian War of 1879. What was his name?

A: Ouray (1833-1880). He is said to have shot tribesmen who opposed his views.

Q: What Nez Perce Indian leader was called the Indian Napoleon?

A: Chief Joseph.

———————?ι ———————

Q: What does *nez perce* mean in English?

A: "Pierced nose." French trappers in the Pacific Northwest named them for the ornaments they wore in their noses.

———————?ι ———————

Q: The Battle of White Bird Creek, Idaho Territory, June 17, 1877, pitted Capt. David Perry of the First Cavalry and just over one hundred troops against Chief Joseph and sixty-five, or so, Nez Perce Indians. What was the outcome?

A: The army suffered thirty-three troops and one officer killed, plus four others wounded. The Nez Perce suffered no deaths and only three wounded.

———————?ι ———————

Q: Why was the Battle at White Bird important?

A: It brought together the five non-treaty bands of the Nez Perce who were then able to resist capture by the army for three and one-half months.

———————?ι ———————

Q: What famous line did Chief Joseph (1840-1904) utter when he surrendered to Col. Nelson Miles and Gen. O. O. Howard on October 5, 1877, at Snake Creek, Montana?

A: "I am tired. My heart is sick and sad. From where the sun now stands I will fight no more forever."

———————?ι ———————

Q: Where was home to the Maricopa and Pima Indian people during the nineteenth century?

A: Central Arizona.

Q: When was the first fight at Adobe Walls, Texas?

A: Kit Carson and a 250 man troop of Volunteers, accompanied by a few regulars with two mountain howitzers, fought 2,000 to 3,000 Indians, Kiowas, Comanches, Arapahoes and Apaches, at the Adobe Walls in November of 1864.

———————?¿ ———————

Q: What was the outcome of the first fight at Adobe Walls?

A: Colonel Carson was able to retreat, his rear protected by the mountain howitzers, to a supply train which had been following his troops. The Indians chose not to press the attack at that point. Carson lost six dead and twenty-two wounded. Indian losses were estimated at 50 to 150.

———————?¿ ———————

Q: Can a comparison be drawn between the first fight at Adobe Walls, Texas, and the Battle at Little Bighorn, Montana, some twelve years later?

A: Yes. The number of troops and the number of Indians were similar at both fights. Colonel Carson, however, respected his enemy and chose to save his men to fight another day.

———————?¿ ———————

Q: What Comanche Chief led the attack in the second battle of Adobe Walls, Texas, in June of 1874?

A: Quanah Parker led an estimated 600 to 700 Comanches, Kiowas and Cheyennes against twenty-eight buffalo hunters (including Bat Masterson) in the second fight at Adobe Walls.

———————?¿ ———————

Q: What was the outcome of the second fight at Adobe Walls?

A: The buffalo hunters suffered three men killed. Countless dozens of Indian attackers were killed. The exact number is not known because the Indians carried away some of their dead. More than a dozen Indians, however, were left on the field after the final retreat.

————————?¿————————

Q: What gave the buffalo hunters such an advantage at the second Battle of the Adobe Walls?

A: They were armed with high-powered Sharps rifles, some fitted with telescopic sights. They could pick off the Indians at random, at long range. One story told is that a hunter shot and killed an Indian at nearly 1,500 yards, about eight-tenths of a mile.

————————?¿————————

Q: What was the far-reaching result of the devastating defeat of the Indians at the second fight at Adobe Walls?

A: The Indians went on a rampage of murder and mutilation, rape and robbery, of whites, including men, women and children. They attacked farms and ranches, travelers and mail carriers, throughout the region, killing all with whom they came into contact. The Great White Father in Washington then declared war on the Indians, the so-called Red River War of 1874-1875.

————————?¿————————

Q: Gen. Phil Sheridan's strategy in the Red River War was total war. What was its result?

A: In the late summer of 1874, assaults were launched on the Indians from all directions by army troops. Villages were overrun and destroyed, supplies captured and horses killed. By the spring of 1875, most of the Indians had capitulated. Nearly seventy-five leaders of the Comanche, Kiowa, Cheyenne, Arapaho and Caddo were shipped off to Florida in chains. Quanah Parker was not one of them.

Photo courtesy of Panhandle-Plains Historical Museum, Canyon, Texas

Q: Who was this chief who led an attack by Comanche, Kiowa, and Cheyenne Indians against buffalo hunters at the Adobe Walls, Texas, in June of 1874?

A: The Comanche Quanah Parker (1845-1911). While he surrendered to the army at Fort Sill in 1875 and adopted the white man's ways, he was an active and ardent supporter of Comanche causes for the remainder of his life.

Q: Who was Quanah Parker's mother?

A: Nine-year-old Cynthia Ann Parker was captured by Comanches in 1836 in north Texas. As a young woman, she married a chief named Peta Nocona by whom she had three children -- two boys and a girl.

———————?ῑ———————

Q: After nearly a quarter century with the Comanches, what was Cynthia Ann Parker's fate?

A: She was "rescued" in 1860 and returned to white society. She died not long after her daughter died in 1865.

———————?ῑ———————

Q: Name the Kiowa Indian chief who signed the Medicine Lodge Treaty in Kansas in 1867 but continued his hostile ways until 1874 when he was captured for the last time.

A: Satanta. He is quoted as saying, "I love to roam over the wild prairie. There I am free and happy."

———————?ῑ———————

Q: Why did Satanta, in 1871, set an ambush not far from Fort Richardson, in north-central Texas, and then allow Gen. William T. Sherman and a detachment of troops to pass?

A: A medicine man had told him to wait for the second party to enter the trap. General Sherman passed first. The second party was a supply wagon train which Satanta captured, killing half a dozen teamsters as he did so.

———————?ῑ———————

Q: What became of Satanta as a result of this raid?

A: General Sherman invited him to a parley at Fort Sill, Indian Territory, and then arrested him for murder. Satanta was tried, convicted and sentenced to hang. There was a popular backlash, however, and the chief was released from custody in 1873.

Q: What was the final fate of Satanta?

A: He surrendered at the Darlington Agency, Indian Territory, early in the Red River War, in October 1874. He was sent back to the penitentiary where he committed suicide in March of 1878.

———————?¿———————

Q: What were the names of the two Cheyenne chiefs killed early in the battle at the Washita River in November of 1868 by elements of the Seventh Cavalry?

A: Black Kettle and Little Rock. The Army later claimed that more than one hundred Indians were killed at Washita. The Indians claimed they lost less than twenty.

———————?¿———————

Q: Name some of the other tribes encamped along the Washita River at the time the Cheyenne camp was attacked in November 1868, by the Seventh Cavalry.

A: Arapaho, Kiowa, Comanche and Apache.

———————?¿———————

Q: What Indian tribe was attacked by the U.S. Fourth Cavalry under Col. Ranald S. Mackenzie at Remolino, Coahuila, Mexico, in May of 1873?

A: The Kickapoos. This particular battle was fought mostly against old men, women and children.

———————?¿———————

Q: Where and when was the last major battle of the Indian Wars of the American West fought?

A: It was at Wounded Knee, South Dakota, on December 29, 1890, that an impromptu battle erupted between elements of the U.S. Seventh Cavalry and the Oglala Sioux. "Major" is the key word here. There were minor battles, especially in Texas and Arizona, until 1896.

Q: What was the name of the Sioux Indian Chief whose band was being searched for weapons when the Battle of Wounded Knee erupted?

A: Big Foot. He was killed in the fighting along with about 150 of his tribesmen. Twenty-five soldiers were killed.

————?¿————

Q: Where were the Navajos imprisoned after being defeated by the U.S. Army under Gen. James H. Carleton and Col. Kit Carson in the early 1860s?

A: At the Bosque Redondo on the Pecos River near the present day town of Fort Sumner, New Mexico. The Navajos were held there from 1863 to 1868 when they were allowed to return to their ancestral homeland in northeastern Arizona and northwestern New Mexico.

————?¿————

Q: What did the Great White Father in Washington, D.C., hope to accomplish at Bosque Redondo?

A: This was an experiment in which the Indians were expected to become farmers and thus self-sufficient.

————?¿————

Q: There were an estimated 1,000 United States Army actions against "hostile" North American Indians between 1866 and 1896. How many casualties were suffered by the Indians? How many by the U.S. Army?

A: Such figures, especially regarding Indian casualties, are questionable. One source indicates that more than 4,300 Indians were killed, 1,200 or so, wounded, and more than 10,000 captured. The same source shows about 1,000 soldiers killed and another 1,000 wounded.

————?¿————

Photo courtesy of the Wyoming State Museum

Q: Can you name this Sioux Indian leader who played a prominent role in the defeat of Gen. George A. Custer at the Little Bighorn River, Montana, in 1876?

A: This photo is believed by some folks to be that of Chief Crazy Horse (1849-1877) of the Oglala Sioux. Other folks claim that no white man ever got close enough to Crazy Horse to take his picture.

Q: What Indian leader set up and executed the Fetterman Massacre near Fort Phil Kearny, Dakota Territory, on the Bozeman Trail on December 21, 1866?

A: An Oglala Sioux warrior named Crazy Horse (1849-1877).

———————?¿———————

Q: Name the Oglala Sioux Chief who made eight trips to Washington and points east, beginning in 1870, in an effort to negotiate for the benefit of his people.

A: Red Cloud. He believed that the white man's superior numbers and army would ultimately defeat the Sioux.

———————?¿———————

Q: What Sioux leaders gained influence with their people as Red Cloud's influence faded by the mid 1870s?

A: Sitting Bull, Crazy Horse and Gall.

———————?¿———————

Q: The Minnesota Massacre began on August 17, 1862, when four young Santee Sioux braves killed a settler, his wife and daughter and two family friends. Before it was over on September 23, more than 400 settlers had been killed. How many Indians were hanged for these depredations?

A: More than 307 Indians were sentenced to death. President Lincoln commuted all but thirty-eight of the death sentences and they were hanged on December 26, 1862.

———————?¿———————

Q: Can you name the three Santee Sioux Chiefs, leaders in the Minnesota Massacre, who were not hanged with their tribesmen?

A: They were Little Crow, Shakopee, and Medicine Bottle. Little Crow escaped but was shot to death by a farmer. Shakopee and Medicine Bottle escaped into Canada but were captured and sent back to the U.S. for hanging.

Q: Can you name this Hunkpapa Sioux Indian leader (pictured below) who was killed at Standing Rock, North Dakota, on December 15, 1890?

A: Sitting Bull (1831-1890) and more than half a dozen of his followers were killed by Sioux Indian police officers. A half dozen of the police officers were also killed.

Photo courtesy of the Wyoming State Museum

Q: Sitting Bull was said to be a hero to his people during the 1880s even though he did not personally fight at the Little Big Horn. Why was this?

A: While he did not physically participate, he was an architect of the battle and he helped direct operations.

————?¿————

Q: What were Indian police officers called by their people?

A: "Metal Breasts" because of the badges on their shirtfronts.

————?¿————

Q: Where are the following buried: the Comanche Chief Quanah Parker (and his white mother), the Kiowa Chief Satanta, and the Apache Chief Geronimo?

A: They are all interred at Fort Still, Oklahoma.

————?¿————

Q: Who was the Nevada Paiute Indian who saw God in a vision during an eclipse in 1889, and was instructed in a new religion which involved the five-day ghost dance?

A: Wovoka. The tenets of the new faith, as revealed to him, provided for peace with the white man, the rising of the dead and return of the buffalo herds.

————?¿————

Q: What was the significance of the ghost dance ?

A: Indians wore "ghost shirts" which, they believed, were impervious to bullets. Indian agents and the army worried that the Sioux would have no need of bulletproof shirts unless they planned an armed uprising. This concern led to the Battle of Wounded Knee in 1890.

————?¿————

Q: What was significant about the Indian Appropriations Act passed by congress on March 3, 1871?

A: It abolished the status of Indian tribes as "nations" and decreed that Indians would be considered "individuals." It meant that dealing with the Indians would be based on legislation or executive order rather than by treaty.

CATTLEMEN AND COWBOYS, SHEEPHERDERS AND FARMERS

Agriculture in the Old West

C H A P T E R   5

Q: George McJunkin (1856-1922) was a cowboy and foreman on the Crowfoot Ranch of northeastern New Mexico. What distinguished him from most cowboys of the time?

A: McJunkin was a self-educated black man who carried a telescope with him on horseback so he could examine the nighttime sky. In 1908, he discovered what became known as the Folsom site, where Ice Age men killed now extinct animals 11,000, or so, years ago. He has never been properly recognized for his find.

———?¿———

Q: When did it become possible for farmers to acquire ownership of land in the Old West by simply settling on it?

A: The Homestead Act became law in 1862.

———?¿———

Q: What did the Homestead Act provide?

A: For a small filing fee, anyone could claim a quarter section of land, 160 acres, most of it well west of the ninety-eighth meridian. If the settler stayed on the land, farmed it and "proved it up," it was his (or hers) in five years.

———————?¿———————

Q: When was barbwire first used to fence off the open range in the Old West?

A: Barbwire was developed in 1873, patented and in use by 1874.

———————?¿———————

Q: Who invented it?

A: Joseph F. Glidden of DeKalb, Illinois. By the middle 1880s, more than 100 million pounds of it was being manufactured and sold annually. The days of open ranges in the Old West were over, thanks to a midwestern farmer.

———————?¿———————

Q: In the parlance of the Old West, what were Scutt's Arrow Plate, Brinkerhoff's Splicer, and Decker Spread?

A: Types of barbwire patented in the 1870s and 1880s.

———————?¿———————

Q: Who was Bose Ikard?

A: He was a black cowboy who rode with Charles Goodnight, Oliver Loving, John Chisum, and others. Goodnight had this engraved on Ikard's tombstone in 1929:

> Bose Ikard. Served with me four years on the Goodnight-Loving Trail, never shirked a duty or disobeyed an order, rode with me in many stampedes, participated in three engagements with Comanches, splendid behavior.

———————?¿———————

Photo courtesy of Panhandle-Plains Historical Museum, Canyon, Texas

Q: This Texan began trailing cattle herds north across New Mexico and into Colorado in 1866. By the early 1870s he set up ranching operations in southeastern Colorado along the Arkansas River. What was his name?

A: Charles Goodnight (1836-1929). A former Texas Ranger, he continued ranching operations in the Texas Panhandle, his ranch headquartered at Palo Duro Canyon, south of Amarillo.

Q: "Batwings" are what part of a cowboy's gear?

A: They are a type of chaps (*chaparajos*) of the wraparound variety. That is, they can be put on and taken off without removing boots and spurs.

———————?¿———————

Q: Name two other types of chaps worn by cowboys on the ranges of the Old West.

A: Other types included "shotguns," which were climb-in style, and "woolies" or "grizzles" which were wool or fur-covered and favored by cowhands on the northern ranges.

———————?¿———————

Q: What piece of cowboy equipment's name comes from the Spanish *la reata* or *lazo*?

A: "Lariat" comes from *la reata* and "lasso" comes from *lazo*. *La reata* translates as rope and a *lazo* is a slip knot or snare.

———————?¿———————

Q: What is the origin of the term "buckaroo"?

A: It developed from the Spanish word *vaquero* which means, not surprisingly, "cowboy."

———————?¿———————

Q: What purpose is served by the rows of fancy stitching on the tops of cowboy boots?

A: The stitching reinforces the top and helps keep the leather from blousing down around the ankle.

———————?¿———————

Q: What purpose is served by high heels on cowboy boots?

A: The high heel prevents the foot from slipping through the stirrup and "hanging up." Most injuries sustained by working cowboys occurred when they fell or were thrown from a horse and a foot "hung up" in the rigging.

Photo courtesy of Panhandle-Plains Historical Museum, Canyon, Texas

Q: Can you name this Texas cattleman who drove herds to Illinois in the middle 1850s and to Colorado in the early 1860s before he entered into a short-lived partnership with cattleman Charles Goodnight?

A: Oliver Loving (1812-1867). Loving and Goodnight became partners in 1866 and opened the Goodnight-Loving Trail north from Texas along the Pecos River in eastern New Mexico. Loving died the following year at Fort Sumner after being wounded by Comanche Indians along the Pecos.

Q: New Yorker Richard King (1824-1885) built one of the largest cattle ranches in south Texas beginning in the 1850s. What was his occupation before he got into the cattle business?

A: He was a riverboat captain and a partner in the ownership of a riverboat fleet. Throughout the remainder of his life he was called "Captain."

———?¿———

Q: How much did Richard King pay for the original 15,500 acres which was the beginning of the vast King Ranch at Santa Gertrudis Creek, Texas, in 1853?

A: King purchased the Santa Gertrudis Spanish land grant from the Mendiola family for $300.

———?¿———

Q: How large was the King Ranch by the late 1870s?

A: By then it had grown to about 600,000 acres.

———?¿———

Q: A new breed of beef cattle was developed on the King Ranch in the later part of the 19th century. What was it called?

A: Santa Gertrudis.

———?¿———

Q: Name the rancher, and future president of the United States, who operated the Elkhorn spread on the Little Missouri River in the Dakota Territory in the 1880s.

A: Native New Yorker Theodore Roosevelt (1858-1919) served as president from 1901 to 1909.

———?¿———

Q: What parts of cowboy equipment were and are called "guthooks" or "can openers"?

A: Spurs.

———————?z———————

Q: What are "jinglebobs"?

A: They are small pear-shaped pendants which are loosely attached to the shank of a spur. They serve no purpose except to make the spurs jingle and jangle loudly as the cowboy walks. They are also called "danglers."

———————?z———————

Q: If, as a working cowboy, you were assigned to ride point, swing, flank or drag, in what kind of activity were you engaged?

A: A cattle drive. These were the positions drovers were assigned to keep the herd together and moving.

———————?z———————

Q: On the Texas cattle ranges, beginning in the 1860s, and later on the northern ranges, too, what were "mavericks"?

A: Mavericks were unbranded calves, usually separated from their mothers.

———————?z———————

Q: How did unbranded calves come to be called "mavericks"?

A: They were so-called because of a Texas rancher named Samuel A. Maverick (1803-1870) who did not brand his livestock. When cowboys would find unbranded calves on the range, they would refer to them as "Maverick's" calves. The name caught on.

———————?z———————

Q: Who played the title role in a 1970 movie called *Chisum*?

A: John Wayne (1907-1979).

———————?z———————

Photo courtesy of the Archives/Library, Historical Society for Southeast New Mexico, Roswell, New Mexico

Q: This man was known as "The Pecos Valley Cattle King" and "The Cow King of New Mexico." What was his real name?

A: John S. Chisum (1824-1884).

Q: How big was John Chisum's ranch?

A: In the middle 1870s he controlled a ranch which was 150 miles long north to south, and 100 miles wide east to west. It extended from just south of present day Fort Sumner to south of Roswell along the Pecos River. A hundred cowboys worked for him tending 80,000 head of cattle.

————————?¿————————

Q: Is it correct to say that the horse stock which became cow ponies was introduced to the Old West by the Spaniard Francisco Vasquez de Coronado in 1540?

A: That is generally believed to be the case. The Lakota Sioux, however, maintain that their ancestors used horses long before the Spanish arrived in North America.

————————?¿————————

Q: In cowboy parlance, what was a "remuda"?

A: On the southern cattle ranges, it was the herd of extra horses taken along on a cattle drive or roundups. On the northern ranges it was often called the saddle band.

————————?¿————————

Q: Would it be accurate to say that fully one-half of the cowboys who rode the cattle ranges of the Old West, that is, from the close of the Civil War to the turn of the century, were either black or Hispanic?

A: No, but about one-third of them were.

————————?¿————————

Q: What was the main difference in purpose between Spanish and Mexican *vaqueros*, and the cowboys which followed after the American Civil War?

A: The *vaqueros* tended cattle for consumption locally. The cowboys tended beef cattle sold to a huge national market, especially after the coming of the railroad.

Photo courtesy of the South Dakota State Historical Society

Q: Black cowboy and rodeo rider Nat Love was better known by what name?

A: Deadwood Dick. He claimed to have been given the name after winning a roping contest at Deadwood, Dakota Territory, in 1876. He rode the western ranges from 1869 until the turn of the century.

Q: Name the rodeo cowboy, billed as the "Dusky Demon," who invented the event called bulldogging.

A: Bill Pickett, a black cowboy, was able to wrestle a steer to the ground using only his teeth. He died in 1932 and was admitted to the Rodeo Cowboy Hall of Fame in 1972.

———————?¿———————

Q: Early day rodeos were held in Pecos, Texas (1883), and Prescott, Arizona (1888). What was a major difference between the two?

A: In Prescott, for the first time, spectators were obliged to pay to watch.

———————?¿———————

Q: Name the ranch which covered virtually all of Motley and Dickens Counties in the Texas panhandle in 1888.

A: The Matador Land and Cattle Company amounted to 1,500,000 acres. It also extended well into Cottle and Floyd Counties.

———————?¿———————

Q: The Matador Land and Cattle Company was owned by an association of Scotsmen in Dundee. A Scot, then living in Trinidad, Colorado, was hired to oversee the Matador ranch in 1890. What was his name?

A: Murdo Mackenzie (1850-1939) was considered to have been significant in shaping the cattle industry in the American West, from the days of open ranges through feed lot operations.

———————?¿———————

Q: Who invented the cowboy hat?

A: John B. Stetson (1830-1906) of Philadelphia. While visiting the West in the early 1860s, he recognized the need for a broad-brimmed, high-crowned hat.

Q: What was the "Boss of the Plains"?

A: The first hat marketed by John B. Stetson was called the "Boss of the Plains."

Photo courtesy of the Wyoming State Museum

Q: Name the Old West city in which this structure was located at 120 East 17th Street?

A: Cheyenne, Wyoming. This was the famous Cheyenne Club, a playhouse for the rich cattle barons of the late nineteenth century.

———————?¿———————

Q: Were Levi's jeans originally designed for wear by cowboys?

A: No. By 1853, Strauss was selling them primarily to miners around San Francisco who arrived in California during the Gold Rush which began in 1848.

———?¿———

Q: By the 1870s blue denim britches, made by Levi Strauss (1829?-1902), were available and popular among cowboys. Is this the same garment available today?

A: Not really. All pockets were riveted into place. There were no belt loops but each pair was equipped with suspender buttons, front and back. There was also a cinch strap on the back. Even then, they were "shrink to fit."

———?¿———

Q: How much would a cowboy's double cinch stock saddle weigh?

A: Forty pounds and more, depending on the specific style and accessories.

———?¿———

Q: Name the eastern Montana cattleman who was also a writer, artist, civic leader, and vigilante in the 1880s.

A: Granville Stuart (1835-1919). He went on in life to serve as U.S. Minister to Paraguay and Uruguay.

———?¿———

Q: In 1892, the Wyoming Stock Growers Association decided to rid the northern Wyoming ranges of rustlers, farmers and small ranchers. They hired more than twenty Texas gunmen to do so. What was the confrontation called?

A: Depending on the source, it was called the Johnson County War, The Johnson County Invasion, or Raid, The Rustler's War, or the War on the Powder River.

Q: Johnson County was, and is, located in north central Wyoming. The county seat is Buffalo. How did the Texas gunmen and Wyoming cattlemen plan to conduct their invasion?

A: They planned to cut telegraph wires, isolate and capture Buffalo, assassinate the sheriff and other county officers, and then kill all the people on a long list of suspected cattle thieves. The cattlemen were so arrogant that they allowed newspapermen to accompany the expedition.

———————?———————

Q: Did the Texans and stockmen invading Johnson County ever reach the town of Buffalo?

A: No. Through a series of blunders, misjudgments, and squabbling, the entire group, forty-two strong, found itself holed up at a place called the TA Ranch, about fourteen miles from town, surrounded by 300 local farmers and ranchers, the sheriff, Red Angus, and his deputies.

———————?———————

Q: How was the Johnson County War finally resolved?

A: Three troops of cavalry from nearby Fort McKinney intervened on the morning of April 13, 1892, and the Texans and stockmen were allowed to surrender to them. Ultimately, all charges against the invaders were dropped, and most of the Texans went home.

———————?———————

Q: Who were Nate Champion and Nick Ray?

A: They were cowboys who were staying at the KC ranch, not far off the line of march of the Johnson County invaders. The invaders detoured to attend to Champion and Ray, both of whom they killed from ambush.

———————?———————

BOOMTOWNS AND BACK TRAILS

Geography of the Trans-Mississippi West

CHAPTER 6

Q: What is generally considered the line where the Old West began and the east ended?

A: The ninety-eighth meridian. It occurs just east of San Antonio, Texas, and extends north through central Oklahoma and Kansas, eastern Nebraska, and the Dakotas, just east of Aberdeen.

————————?¿————————

Q: What makes the ninety-eighth meridian the magic demarcation between east and west?

A: Eastern forests end and western grasslands begin by the ninety-eighth meridian. There is also a marked difference in the amount of rainfall, the east receiving much more than the west.

————————?¿————————

Q: What line of demarcation between east and west is used for purposes of this book, and why?

A: The Mississippi River. Jesse James has a place in any consideration of the Old West, and so do Judge Isaac Parker and the Dalton gang, and yet Minnesota, Missouri, Arkansas and Coffeyville, Kansas, are well east of the 98th meridian.

———————?¿———————

Q: What was described as, "Too thin to slice, too thick to drink"?

A: The Missouri River near Fort Leavenworth, Kansas.

———————?¿———————

Q: Was the population of Arizona more or less than 10,000 people in 1870?

A: A little less at 9,658, according to the census. For the sake of comparison, the 1990 population of the state was 3,665,228 souls.

———————?¿———————

Q: Which had the larger population in 1870, Tennessee or Texas?

A: Tennessee by 1,258,520 to 818,579 in all of vast Texas. Ten years later it was almost a dead heat: Tennessee: 1,542,359; Texas: 1,591,749.

———————?¿———————

Q: Name at least three states west of the Mississippi in which you will find a Silver City.

A: Idaho, Iowa, Nevada, New Mexico, South Dakota and Utah. The one in New Mexico is the largest.

———————?¿———————

Q: What town was the seat of Cochise County, Arizona Territory, in 1881?

A: Tombstone.

Q: What was the seat of Lincoln County, New Mexico Territory, in the 1870s during the Lincoln County War.

A: Lincoln. It is now at Carrizozo.

———————?ₜ———————

Q: What state capital has the same name as the county and state in which it is located?

A: Oklahoma City is in Oklahoma County, Oklahoma.

———————?ₜ———————

Q: Where in the Old West will you find a single county which borders upon four states?

A: Cimarron County, Oklahoma, borders on Kansas, Colorado, New Mexico and Texas.

———————?ₜ———————

Q: Is Laramie, Wyoming, the county seat of Laramie County?

A: No. Laramie is the seat of Albany County. Cheyenne is the seat of Laramie County.

———————?ₜ———————

Q: Is Fort Laramie, established in 1834, in Laramie County, Wyoming?

A: No. Fort Laramie is in Goshen County.

———————?ₜ———————

Q: Portland, Oregon, was incorporated on January 23, 1851. For what other city was it named?

A: On the flip of coin it was named for Portland, Maine.

———————?ₜ———————

Q: For whom was Pocatello, Idaho, named?

A: A Shoshoni Indian Chief of the same name who resisted the encroachment of the white man until well into the 1860s. He died in 1884.

Q: What capital of an Old West state is known as "The City Different"?

A: Santa Fe, New Mexico.

———————?ℓ———————

Q: What four territories became states in November 1889?

A: North and South Dakota (November 2), Montana (November 8), and Washington (November 11). They were the 39th, 40th, 41st and 42nd states admitted to the Union.

———————?ℓ———————

Q: What did Mormon leader and pioneer Brigham Young (1801-1877) remark upon first seeing the Valley of the Great Salt Lake?

A: "This is the place!" Another source reports that the actual phrase was, "This is the right place."

———————?ℓ———————

Q: When did Brigham Young and his party, amounting to fewer than 150 souls, reach the Valley of Great Salt Lake?

A: July 24, 1847.

———————?ℓ———————

Q: What New Mexico railroad town was originally called Six-Shooter Siding?

A: Tucumcari, in the east central part of the state, was founded in 1902.

———————?ℓ———————

Q: Would it be accurate to say that the sawmills around Puget Sound, Washington, were producing well over 150 million board feet of lumber per year as early as 1869?

A: Yes.

———————?ℓ———————

Q: Built by Charles and William Bent in 1833, Bent's Fort was a trading post and landmark on the Santa Fe Trail in southeastern Colorado along the banks of the Arkansas River. What ever became of it?

A: Charles Bent was killed by Taos Indians in 1847. Brother William continued to operate it until 1849, after which he destroyed it. One source says he blew it up in 1852 because the U.S. Army would not meet his price for it.

———————?¿———————

Q: Name the town where the Jesse James gang met its Waterloo on September 7, 1876.

A: The James gang attempted to rob the First National Bank at Northfield, Minnesota.

———————?¿———————

Q: What was the result of the attempted bank robbery at Northfield?

A: Eight bank robbers rode into town that afternoon. Clel Miller and Bill Chadwell died on the streets of the town, shot by citizens. A posse later chased down and captured the Younger brothers, Cole, Jim and Bob, and killed Charlie Pitts. Only Jesse and Frank James escaped death or prison. Three townsmen were killed in the fight.

———————?¿———————

Q: Is it correct to say that the Idaho potato was developed specifically for the soil in the state of Idaho?

A: No. The Idaho potato was developed by Luther Burbank (1849-1926) in Massachusetts in 1872.

———————?¿———————

Q: Where in California did Luther Burbank set up shop in 1875?

A: Santa Rosa.

Q: What mineral produced the all-time greatest wealth in the history of Nevada mining: gold, silver, copper or lead?

A: Copper.

———————?¿ ———————

Q: What Idaho town was the site of the single largest silver strike in American history?

A: Wallace, Idaho, has been a major mining center since 1884.

———————?¿ ———————

Q: Name the famous actress who was born in Wallace, Idaho.

A: Lana Turner was born there on February 8, 1920.

———————?¿ ———————

Q: What state in the Old West went "dry" in 1880?

A: Kansas, thanks to the efforts of the Women's Christian Temperance Union (WCTU).

———————?¿ ———————

Q: What was the first capital of the Montana Territory, carved out of the Idaho territory in May of 1864?

A: Bannack.

———————?¿ ———————

Q: When Wyoming Territory was created in 1868, it was carved out of what two other territories?

A: Dakota and Utah.

———————?¿ ———————

Q: What city was home to the famed Comstock Lode, discovered in 1859?

A: Virginia City, Nevada.

Q: For whom is the city of Greeley, Colorado, named?

A: New York *Tribune* editor Horace Greeley (1811-1872). The town was formed as an agricultural colony in 1870 by Nathan Meeker who had served as the *Tribune's* agricultural editor. Population by 1880 was about 1,200. In 1990 it was more than 60,000.

———————?¿———————

Q: What prompted the popularity of the slogan, "Pike's Peak or Bust" in 1859?

A: The discovery of gold at Clear Creek (or Boulder Canyon) in January of that year.

———————?¿———————

Q: What happened to a large number of the hearty souls who set out early for the promised gold fields of Colorado in 1859?

A: Estimates are that of the 100,000 or so goldseekers who set out for Colorado that year, half died, or were killed by Indians, got lost, turned back or otherwise gave up.

———————?¿———————

Q: What was the name of the prospector who discovered the gold lode in the Creede/Cripple Creek area of Colorado in 1890?

A: Crazy Bob Womack spent twelve years in locating the vein. He called his mine the El Paso.

———————?¿———————

Q: How rich did Crazy Bob get from the El Paso Mine?

A: Not very. About 1893, he got drunk and sold the mine for $300. The mine ultimately brought in $3,000,000 in gold. Womack died broke in 1909.

———————?¿———————

97

Photo courtesy of W.H. Over Museum, University of South Dakota

Q: Typical of towns which boomed on America's western frontier during the last half of the nineteenth century, can you name this one?

A: This is Deadwood, South Dakota, in 1876, when J. B. Hickok met his demise there.

Q: What ever became of Henry T. P. Comstock for whom the famed lode is named?

A: He sold his share in the Ophir mine (which ultimately produced more than $10,000,000 in ore) for $11,000 and promptly lost it in a business venture. He committed suicide in Bozeman, Montana, in 1870.

———————?¿———————

Q: What were standard wages paid to miners working underground in the mines around Virginia City, Nevada, in the 1870s?

A: They were paid four dollars for an eight-hour work day. They were among the best paid American workers of the time. A top cowhand at the time made $30.00 to $50.00 per month, and he worked from daylight to dark.

———————?¿———————

Q: Can you name the pioneer photographer who shot copious photos of the Old West in the late 1860s and early 1870s, including some taken in the bowels of the Comstock Lode in 1867?

A: Timothy O'Sullivan (1840-1882) was a student of, and assistant to, famed Civil War photographer Mathew Brady (1823-1896).

———————?¿———————

Q: Where did Bob Fitzsimmons become heavyweight boxing champion of the world?

A: He knocked out James J. "Gentleman Joe" Corbett in the fourteenth round at Carson City, Nevada, on March 17, 1897.

———————?¿———————

Q: Is it correct to say that the world's first oil well was drilled near Eureka, California, in 1861?

A: No. The first oil well in the world came in on August 28, 1859, at Titusville, Pennsylvania. The Eureka well, however, was the first in California.

———————?¿———————

Q: Fur trapper turned trader Bill Sublette (1799-1845) and some others purchased a large tract of land at a place called Westport Landing in what is now western Missouri, and subdivided it. What city is located there today?

A: Kansas City.

———————?¿———————

Q: What western territory's first prison was constructed of adobe bricks in 1855 and reduced to near rubble by prisoners by 1857?

A: Utah's. It was called the Mud Prison. This was the same prison which had no guards at night. The day guards simply locked up the prisoners in the evening and went home. Many prisoners had no difficulty in escaping.

———————?¿———————

Q: What town was home to Montana's first territorial prison?

A: Deer Lodge. It was completed in 1870 and by 1874 housed twenty-four convicts in its fourteen cells.

———————?¿———————

Q: The "escape-proof" prison at Santa Fe, New Mexico, opened on August 13, 1885. When did the first successful escapes from it take place?

A: On August 13, 1885. Three prisoners walked away and were never recaptured. Four prisoners had previously escaped in February 1885, while working on construction of the prison. Only one of them was ever recaptured.

———————?¿———————

Q: Where was the first Wyoming territorial prison?

A: It was built at Laramie in 1872 and received its first prisoners in early 1873. During its first two years of service, one out of every four prisoners escaped.

———————?₂———————

Q: George Armstrong Custer's Seventh Cavalry attacked a body of Cheyenne and Arapaho Indians under Chief Black Kettle at the Washita River on November 27, 1868. Where was, and is, the Washita River?

A: In 1868, it was called the Indian Territory. Since November 16, 1907, it has been called Oklahoma. The attack referred to here took place near Oklahoma's border with the Texas panhandle.

———————?₂———————

Q: Butch Cassidy's Wild Bunch was sometimes called the Hole in the Wall Gang. Where was the Hole in the Wall?

A: It was in central Wyoming, north of the middle fork of the Powder River.

———————?₂———————

Q: Another stop on the outlaw trail sometimes used by Cassidy and his cohorts was called Brown's Hole. Where was it located?

A: It was located near the point where Colorado, Utah and Wyoming share a common border, but most maps show it in far northwest Colorado.

———————?₂———————

Q: In July of 1832, there was a battle between several hundred fur trappers and a large body of Gros Ventre Indians at a place called Pierre's Hole, named for Pierre Tivanitagon, in which twenty-six Indians and thirty-two trappers were killed. Where is Pierre's Hole?

A: In Teton County in eastern Idaho, just west of Grand Teton National Park, Wyoming.

———————?ᵫ———————

Q: Where in the Old West was gold discovered on January 24, 1848?

A: In a millrace at a John Sutter's sawmill, near what would become Coloma, on the American River, east of the present day Sacramento, California.

———————?ᵫ———————

Q: Who actually found the gold?

A: James Wilson Marshall of New Jersey, who was in California by way of Oregon. Marshall had supervised construction of the sawmill.

———————?ᵫ———————

Q: Did John Sutter (1803-1880) and James Marshall (1812-1884) profit from the discovery of gold by Marshall on Sutter's property in 1848?

A: Nearly $100 million in gold was extracted in the next twenty-five or so years, but none of it accrued to Sutter or Marshall. They both died poor.

———————?ᵫ———————

Q: What were the people called who migrated to California during the gold rush of 1849? (A hint: "goldseekers," "prospectors" and "forty-niners" are all wrong.)

A: They were called Argonauts.

———————?ᵫ———————

Q: What was the ratio of "respectable women" to prostitutes in the San Francisco of the early 1850s?

A: Prostitutes were outnumbered by about four to one.

———————?ᵫ———————

Q: What major West Coast city suffered at least six major conflagrations between Christmas 1849, and the summer of 1851?

A: San Francisco. The town was a random collection of wooden structures which allowed fire to spread quickly.

———————?———————

Q: What other West Coast city suffered a major fire in June of 1889 which destroyed about fifty blocks of wood structures?

A: Seattle.

———————?———————

Q: What Old West community was called "The City of the Saints"?

A: Salt Lake City. Sir Richard Burton, a British adventurer and writer visited the Mormon capital in 1860 and wrote a book on the Church of Jesus Christ of the Latter-Day Saints called *The City of the Saints and Across the Rocky Mountains to California.*

———————?———————

Q: There are cities in both Nevada and New Mexico called Las Vegas. What does *las vegas* mean in English?

A: "The meadows."

———————?———————

Q: Can you name the New Mexican who discovered the meadow which became Las Vegas, Nevada, in 1829?

A: Antonio Armijo is said to have been looking for a shortcut to Los Angeles on the Old Spanish Trail. He is believed to be the first European to visit what would become Las Vegas, Nevada.

———————?———————

Q: Where in the West will you find the Rough Riders Memorial and City Museum?

A: Las Vegas, New Mexico. Teddy Roosevelt recruited many of his Rough Riders in New Mexico.

———————?———————

Photo courtesy of the Denver Public Library, Western History Department

Q: This was one of the most famous cow towns in the Kansas frontier. Can you name it?

A: Dodge City in the middle to late 1870s.

———————?———————

Q: Some estimates place the number of buffalo on the western plains of North America at 15,000,000 to 20,000,000 during the first half of the nineteenth century. How many of the great beasts were left by the middle 1890s?

A: Less than 1,000 head. In 1872-1873 alone, 1.25 million buffalo hides were shipped east by rail. The carcasses were left on the plains to rot.

———————?¿———————

Q: Deaf Smith County is located in the Panhandle of West Texas. For whom was it named?

A: Erastus "Deaf" Smith, was indeed hard of hearing, but that didn't stop him from service as a scout for Sam Houston against the Mexican Army in 1836. He is said to have been one of Houston's most trusted aides.

———————?¿———————

Q: What old southwestern territorial prison was located on the banks of the Colorado River, only twenty-six miles from the Mexico border?

A: The Arizona territorial prison at Yuma confined its first prisoners in July of 1876. It would accommodate a maximum of thirty-two prisoners at the time.

———————?¿———————

Q: How long did the Arizona Territorial prison at Yuma remain in use?

A: It was abandoned as a prison in 1909. The prison hospital was used as a high school for a short period and then it was left to decay. It is now an historical monument.

———————?¿———————

Q: In what community in far west Texas would you find a saloon called the Jersey Lily in the 1880s and 1890s?

A: Langtry, named by Judge Roy Bean (1825-1903) for actress Lillie Langtry (1852-1929) in 1882.

———————?——————

Q: There was a prizefight between Bob Fitzsimmons and Peter Maher in February of 1896. Where in the Old West did it take place?

A: On an island in the Rio Grande south of El Paso. Boxing had been outlawed in both the State of Texas and the Territory of New Mexico, so Judge Roy Bean promoted the fight on the island which might have belonged to Mexico. Fitzsimmons knocked Maher out in ninety-five seconds of the first round.

———————?——————

Q: What central Oklahoma city went from a population of zero to more than 10,000 people in a little more than a single day in April of 1889?

A: Guthrie. The town site stood in the path of the race for land when the Indian Territory was officially opened for settlement on April 22, 1889.

———————?——————

Q: For whom is Pike's Peak, Colorado, named?

A: Zebulon Montgomery Pike (1779-1813) who reached the Colorado Rockies during the winter of 1806-1807.

———————?——————

Q: When Zebulon Pike wrote in 1807, "[They looked] exactly like . . . a sea in a storm, except as to the color," to what was he referring?

A: The Great Sand Dunes of south central Colorado.

———————?——————

Q: Where in the Old West was Fort Fizzle, and why was it so named?

A: It was in the Bitterroot Valley of western Montana. It was there that Captain Charles Rawn set up a barricade to stop the Nez Perce Indians on their retreat from the Wallowa Mountains in Oregon. The Indians slipped around the barricade and proceeded on their way. Local folks called the place Fort Fizzle.

———————?———————

Q: What happened at Truckee Lake in the Sierra Nevada of eastern California on October 31, 1846?

A: The Donner Party was halted by deep snows on its westward trek over the Truckee pass to the Sacramento Valley.

———————?———————

Q: The end of October was late in the season to attempt to cross the Sierra Nevada in the days of the pioneers. Why was the Donner party attempting it at that time?

A: They set off from Fort Bridger, Utah Territory, at the end of July over the Hastings Cutoff, a trail which was supposed to be 400 miles shorter than the regular Oregon and California trails. The route was untested and untried. It took them eleven weeks to reach the Sierra Nevada whereas parties which followed the normal route made the trip in eight weeks. The three-week delay was catastrophic.

———————?———————

Q: What became of the Donner Party?

A: Of the eighty-one pioneers trapped at Truckee Lake on October 31, forty-seven survived, many of them by resorting to cannibalism.

———————?———————

107

Q: What was called the Truckee Pass in the California Sierra Nevada in 1846 is now known by what name?

A: Donner Pass.

―――――*?¿*―――――

Q: When was Yosemite National Park originally set aside as a preserve?

A: It was designated for special protection by the State of California in 1864. It became a national park in 1890.

―――――*?¿*―――――

Q: When did Yellowstone become the nation's first National Park?

A: 1879.

―――――*?¿*―――――

Q: Where in the Old West was a soft drink called Dr. Pepper introduced to a thirsty public in 1885?

A: Wade Morrison's Corner Drug Store in Waco, Texas.

―――――*?¿*―――――

Q: Where is there seldom heard a discouraging word?

A: "Home on the Range," written in 1873 by Brewster Higley, music by Dan Kelley, is the Kansas state song.

―――――*?¿*―――――

WAGON TRAINS, STAGECOACHES AND THE IRON HORSE

Transportation & Communication in the Old West

CHAPTER 7

Q: The Pony Express began operations on April 3, 1860, moving mail between St. Joseph, Missouri, and Sacramento, California. How long did it operate after that?

A: The last Pony Express rider delivered his mailbag in San Francisco on November 20, 1861, one year, seven months, two weeks and three days later.

———?¿———

Q: How long did the Pony Express advertise that it would take to deliver mail from St. Joseph to Sacramento, and vice versa?

A: Ten days. The first run west from St. Joseph actually took nine days and twenty-two hours.

———?¿———

Q: What was the Wells Fargo postage on a half-ounce letter over the Pony Express, from one end to the other?

A: $1.00. U.S. Postage was also required.

————————?ι————————

Q: What brought about the demise of the Pony Express?

A: The completion of the transcontinental telegraph line at Salt Lake City on October 24, 1861.

————————?ι————————

Q: What were the "ships of the desert" which had but a brief popularity on the western frontier?

A: Camels.

————————?ι————————

Q: Who was commander of the U. S. Army's Camel Corps?

A: Lt. Edward F. "Ned" Beale (1822-1893) helped convince the U.S. Army that camels were the transportation wave of the future. In 1856, seventy-five of the creatures were purchased in Tunis and shipped to Texas. A year later, Beale took them to California via a circuitous route, and a year after that, the whole experiment was mostly forgotten.

————————?ι————————

Q: What became of the camels?

A: Beale "adopted" some of them from the army. Some were sold to zoos and circuses. Others wandered the deserts of Arizona and New Mexico for years, often startling those who happened to come across them. Two of them were reported seen as late as 1907 in Nevada.

————————?ι————————

Q: How much was the stagecoach fare from Independence, Missouri, to Santa Fe, New Mexico, in the 1850s?

A: About $250.00.

———————?𝑖———————

Q: At what rate of speed did a celerity stagecoach travel on the old Butterfield mail route between Missouri and California?

A: They averaged about five miles an hour over the entire route. They ran twenty-four hours per day.

———————?𝑖———————

Q: At what rate of speed did a pioneer wagon train travel?

A: Two miles per hour was a brisk clip. Twelve to fifteen miles per day was considered average.

———————?𝑖———————

Q: Under what different circumstances were four- and six-horse teams used to pull stagecoaches?

A: Six-horse teams were used over mountain routes, as much for their braking power going downhill as their strength in pulling the coach uphill. Four-horse teams were used for speed, and with frequent horse changes, they could make up to eight miles per hour.

———————?𝑖———————

Q: John Butterfield (1801-1860?) contracted with the U.S. Post Office in 1857 to haul the mail from St. Louis, Missouri, to San Francisco, California, in what period of time?

A: Twenty-five days. The stagecoach was actually able to make the trip in twenty-three days, twenty-three and one-half hours. Butterfield's $600,000 per year contract lasted for just under two years (two years, five months and seventeen days) until the beginning of the Civil War.

———————?𝑖———————

Q: The American Express Company was formed by a merger of what two transportation companies in 1850?

A: The Butterfield Overland Mail Company and Wells, Fargo & Company. Henry Wells (1805-1878) and William George Fargo (1818-1881) forced John Butterfield out of the company by 1860.

———————?ℓ———————

Q: The southern Butterfield Overland mail route between St. Louis and San Francisco, which passed through El Paso, Texas, and Tucson, Arizona, was called what?

A: The Oxbow Route.

———————?ℓ———————

Q: In 1848, Missouri's U.S. Sen. Thomas Hart Benton (1782-1858), with the help of some of his wealthy friends, commissioned the survey of a line which would run roughly along the thirty-eighth parallel over which the railroad could travel from St. Louis to San Francisco. Who led the surveying expedition?

A: Senator Benton's son-in-law, John C. Fremont (1813-1890).

———————?ℓ———————

Q: What was Fremont's nickname?

A: He was known as "The Pathfinder" for his many treks into the American West.

———————?ℓ———————

Q: Was Fremont successful in finding a viable route for the railroad along the thirty-eighth parallel across the trans-Mississippi west?

A: In spite of the fact that he and his party were stranded by deep snows in the Rocky Mountains and nearly a dozen of his men died, and he himself was only saved by friendly Indians, Fremont called the result " . . . entirely satisfactory."

———————?ℓ———————

Q: Where and when was the first transcontinental railroad completed?

A: Promontory Point, Utah, May 10, 1869. The route was well north of the thirty-eighth parallel.

———?¿———

Q: How many railroad spikes were driven during the ceremonies celebrating the completion of the first transcontinental railroad?

A: There were four spikes: two were gold, one was silver and one was an alloy of gold, silver and iron. None of them were driven. They were simply dropped into pre-drilled holes by celebrities in attendance.

———?¿———

Q: Who was president of the Central Pacific Railroad at the time it joined the Union Pacific at Promontory Point in 1869?

A: Leland Stanford (1824-1893). He also served as governor (1861-1863) and U. S. Senator (1885-1893) from California.

———?¿———

Q: Leland Stanford made a fortune off the railroad. What did he do with a portion of his wealth?

A: He founded Stanford University near San Francisco in 1885.

———?¿———

Q: Where and when was the second transcontinental railroad completed?

A: A silver spike was driven connecting the Southern Pacific (SP) and the Atchison, Topeka and Santa Fe (AT&SF) Railroads at Deming, New Mexico, on March 8, 1881.

———?¿———

Q: What railroad was completed at Gold Creek, Montana, on September 8, 1883?

A: The Northern Pacific. Approval of the construction of the line dated back to the Abraham Lincoln administration in 1864. A German by the name of Henry Villard saw to the completion of it.

———————?i ———————

Q: What transcontinental railroad, completed on September 18, 1893, was built without government subsidies?

A: The Great Northern Railroad.

———————?i ———————

Q: Who was responsible for the completion of the Great Northern Railroad?

A: Canadian born James Jerome "J. J." Hill (1838-1916) was the driving force behind it.

———————?i ———————

Q: There was a race between the Atchison, Topeka and Santa Fe (AT&SF) Railway and the Denver and Rio Grande (D&RG) Railway for use of the Raton Pass between Colorado and New Mexico. Who won?

A: The AT&SF won and the first train entered New Mexico on December 7, 1878.

———————?i ———————

Q: In what year did the famed Santa Fe Trail open trade between the United States and Mexico, between Franklin, Missouri, and Santa Fe, *Nuevo Mejico*?

A: 1821.

———————?i ———————

Q: What momentous political change in the Spanish Southwest made trade over the Santa Fe Trail possible?

A: Mexico's (including New Mexico's) independence from Spain in 1821. The Spanish had been isolationists while the Mexicans in New Mexico were anxious for trade with the United States.

———?ᵪ———

Q: Who first opened the Santa Fe Trail as a trade route?

A: William Becknell (1790-1832) left Franklin, Missouri in the fall of 1821 with a pack train of trade goods. He returned the following year considerably enriched, thus generating a great deal of interest in trade with New Mexico.

———?ᵪ———

Q: How many states did the Santa Fe Trail traverse when it opened for trade?

A: Actually, only one, Missouri, which was admitted to the Union in 1821. The others did not become states until much later. In modern terms, it crossed parts of Missouri, Kansas, Oklahoma, Colorado and New Mexico.

———?ᵪ———

Q: The southern, and most direct, branch of the Santa Fe Trail, which crossed the Cimarron River in southwestern Kansas, was called what?

A: The Cimarron Cutoff. It held the advantage of being shorter and taking a little less time. Its disadvantages had to do with the scarcity of water and the danger of attacks from Comanches, Kiowas, Arapahos and/or Cheyennes.

———?ᵪ———

Q: The northern, and longer, route of the Santa Fe Trail, which avoided Oklahoma completely and entered New Mexico from Colorado over the Raton Pass, was called what?

A: The Mountain Route. It offered the advantage of abundant water and a layover at Bent's Fort in southeastern Colorado.

———————?ι ———————

Q: What was the difference in distance over the two routes of the Santa Fe Trail?

A: The Mountain Route was 909 miles. The Cimarron Cutoff was 865 miles, for a net difference of forty-four miles.

———————?ι ———————

Q: The Mountain Route and the Cimarron Cutoff parted ways just to the west of Fort Dodge, Kansas. Where did they rejoin to become a single trail into Santa Fe, New Mexico?

A: Near Fort Union in northeastern New Mexico.

———————?ι ———————

Q: Francois Xavier Aubry was a trader over the Santa Fe Trail. What did he do in 1848 which established an unheard of record, and made headlines?

A: Using relays of horses, he rode from Santa Fe, New Mexico, to Independence, Missouri, a distance of eight hundred miles, in five days and thirteen hours. (Some other sources claim it was actually five days and sixteen hours.) Under normal circumstances, such a trip on horseback would take two or three weeks.

———————?ι ———————

Q: How long would the trip from Independence to Santa Fe, via the Cimarron Cutoff, take using a six mule team pulling a wagon laden with personal baggage and household goods?

A: About forty days. Such a rig, under normal circumstances, could average about twenty miles per day.

————————?¿————————

Q: What brought about the demise of the Santa Fe Trail as an important trade link between the markets in the East and the markets in the Southwest?

A: The first railroad tracks from the east traversed the Raton Pass in 1878, and arrived in Santa Fe in February, 1880. Freight could be moved much more efficiently by rail and the need for the overland trade route ended.

————————?¿————————

Q: What was the trade route from Mexico City to Santa Fe, via Chihuahua and Paseo del Norte, called?

A: *El Camino Real* (The Royal Road).

————————?¿————————

Q: There was a shortcut on *El Camino Real* in *Nuevo Mejico*. It lay to the east of the Rio Grande and extended from Rincon to San Marcial across ninety waterless miles of desert. What was it called?

A: *El Jornada del Muerto* (The Route of the Dead Man or the Journey of the Dead).

————————?¿————————

Q: Why was *El Jornada del Muerto* so called?

A: One story goes that a German by the name of Gruber was found dead along the trail in the late seventeenth century, hence "Route of the Dead Man." However, estimates are that nearly 1,000 men, women and children died on this road in the early years, so the more generic "Journey of the Dead" seems more appropriate.

————————?¿————————

Q: What was the name of the trail which left Santa Fe to the northwest, into the Utah Territory, and then back to the southwest, terminating in Los Angeles?

A: The Old Spanish Trail.

———————?———————

Q: Where was the first permanent trading post established in Wyoming?

A: William Sublette (1799-1845) and Robert Campbell established a trading post near the confluence of the Laramie and North Platte Rivers in 1834 and called it Fort William. After they sold it, the name was changed to Fort John. When the American Fur Co. bought it, it became Fort Laramie in 1834.

———————?———————

Q: What ever became of Fort Laramie?

A: It became a stop on the Oregon Trail in 1840 and the U.S. Army bought it in 1849. It was abandoned as a military post in 1890. It is now a national historical site.

———————?———————

Q: What were the last two of the Old West Territories to be admitted to the Union?

A: New Mexico (January 6, 1912) and Arizona (February 14, 1912). It could be argued, but not very convincingly, that they were Alaska (January 3, 1959) and Hawaii (August 21, 1959).

———————?———————

GOVERNORS, JUDGES AND OTHER POLITICIANS

Some Statesmen & Some Blackguards in the Old West

CHAPTER 8

Q: Who wrote the famous line, "Go west, young man, go west"?

A: John Babsone Lane Soule (1815-1891) wrote it in the Terre Haute (Indiana) *Express* in 1851.

―――――?₂―――――

Q: Why is newspaper editor and presidential candidate (1872) Horace Greeley (1811-1872) so often credited with the above line?

A: Greeley did write, " . . . turn your face to the great West, and there build up a home and fortune." He also often offered the "go west" advice to young men. Greeley credited Soule with having coined the phrase.

―――――?₂―――――

Q: Can you name the U.S. Congressman who said in the 1890s, "The people of Nebraska are for free silver. Therefore, I am for free silver. I'll look up the reasons later."

A: William Jennings Bryan (1860-1925).

———————?ι———————

Q: Who said of the American West in 1845:
What do we want with this region of savages and wild beasts, of deserts, of shifting sands and whirlwinds of dust, of cactus and prairie dogs . . . with the western coast line three thousand miles away, rockbound, cheerless and uninviting?

A: U.S. Sen. Daniel Webster (1782-1852) of Massachusetts. He also opposed coast-to-coast postal service. "I will never vote one cent from the public treasury to place the Pacific Coast one inch closer to Boston than it is now." (1838)

———————?ι———————

Q: What federal bureaucracy was created under President James Monroe on June 17, 1824?

A: The Bureau of Indian Affairs was created under the War Department. It was not placed under the Interior Department until 1849.

———————?ι———————

Q: Who was the Territorial Governor of Arizona at the time of the Gunfight at the O.K. Corral on October 25, 1881?

A: Explorer and Gen. John C. Fremont (1813-1890).

———————?ι———————

Q: What New Mexico Territorial Governor offered a $500 reward for the capture of Billy the Kid in 1880?

A: Author and General Lew Wallace (1827-1905).

———————?ι———————

Q: Who was the first governor of the Utah Territory in 1850?

A: Brigham Young (1801-1877).

Photo courtesy of the Utah State Historical Society

Q: This man was the leader of the first band of Mormon pioneers to reach the Valley of the Great Salt Lake, Utah, on July 24, 1847. What was his name?

A: Brigham Young (1801-1877). "This is the place!" he exclaimed when he saw the valley for the first time.

—————?ι—————

Q: Who was elected the first president of the Republic of Texas in 1836?

A: Sam Houston (1793-1863).

———————?¿———————

Q: Name the so-called "Hanging Judge" who condemned more than 160 men to death during his twenty-one year tenure (1875-1896) on the bench at Fort Smith, Arkansas.

A: Judge Isaac Charles Parker (1839-1896).

———————?¿———————

Q: Of the men condemned to death by Judge Parker, how many were actually hanged?

A: Eighty-eight were actually hanged. (Another source says it was only seventy-nine.) Of the others, some had their sentences commuted by the President of the United States, some were shot while trying to escape and others died in prison.

———————?¿———————

Q: How many of Judge Parker's Federal deputies, who rode the Indian Territory in search of killers and thieves, were themselves killed in the line of duty between 1875 and 1895?

A: Sixty-five.

———————?¿———————

Q: What was the claim to fame of German immigrant George Maledon of Fort Smith, Arkansas, during the last quarter of the nineteenth century?

A: He was the chief executioner for the Western District of Arkansas. He carried out sixty executions for the court of Judge Isaac Parker.

———————?¿———————

Q: Who called himself the "Law West of the Pecos" with some justification?

A: Judge Roy Bean (1826-1903). As Justice of the Peace, he was the only semblance of law from the Pecos River to the Rio Grande in west Texas from the early 1880s until the end of the century.

————————?¿————————

Q: Who played the title role in the 1972 movie, *The Life and Times of Judge Roy Bean*?

A: Paul Newman.

————————?¿————————

Q: What was the untimely fate of Col. Albert Jennings Fountain, judge and frontier prosecuting attorney from Las Cruces, New Mexico, and his son, Henry, in January of 1896?

A: Both of them disappeared somewhere near the White Sands, east of Las Cruces. Their bodies were never found. A great deal of political intrigue surrounded this unfortunate event.

————————?¿————————

Q: Name the New Mexico Territorial Attorney General and District Judge who went on to the U.S. Senate and then served as U.S. Secretary of the Interior before he was convicted of taking bribes in the Teapot Dome, Wyoming, oil scandal and was sentenced to prison.

A: Albert Bacon Fall (1861-1944).

————————?¿————————

Q: Who was the first governor of the State of Texas?

A: James Pinckney Henderson (1808-1858). He served from 1846 to 1848. He also served as Texas' U.S. Senator from 1857 until his death in Washington in 1858.

Photo courtesy of the Utah State Historical Society

Q: Pictured is the first governor of Utah after statehood. Can you name him?

A: Heber M. Wells served as governor from 1896 to 1905.

———————?¿———————

Q: What Utah Territorial Governor declined to give outlaw Butch Cassidy (Robert Leroy Parker) a pardon or amnesty in 1899?

A: Heber M. Wells.

———————?ᵢ———————

Q: There was a political campaign for governor of Texas in 1857 between Sam Houston and Hardin Runnels, a planter and career politician. Who won?

A: Runnels, who strongly supported Texas secession from the United States, beat Houston, who strongly opposed it, by nearly 9,000 votes. Houston ran against Runnels again in 1859 and won by nearly 9,000 votes.

———————?ᵢ———————

Q: Who was the Governor of Wyoming at the time of the Johnson County War in the early 1890s?

A: Amos Barber served as governor from 1890-1893. He favored the stockmen and their hired Texas gunslingers and delayed asking for help from the army until the stockmen requested it.

———————?ᵢ———————

Q: What 1844 Democratic presidential candidate ran on the slogan, "54-40 or fight"?

A: James K. Polk (1795-1849).

———————?ᵢ———————

Q: What did 54-40 mean?

A: 54-40 was the latitude to which the United States claimed the Pacific Northwest. The threat was that the U.S. would go to war to maintain possession that far north. After winning the election, Polk entered into an agreement with England in 1846 which set the line at the forty-ninth parallel.

Q: Who orated, "You shall not press down upon the brow of labor this crown of thorns. You shall not crucify mankind upon a cross of gold," just before he received the Democratic presidential nomination at Chicago in 1896?

A: William Jennings Bryan of Nebraska. He was thirty-six years old at the time.

—————?ι—————

WOMEN OF THE OLD WEST

Saints & Soiled Doves

C H A P T E R   9

Q: Who was known as "Little Sure Shot"?

A: Phoebe Anne Oakley Mozee (1860-1926), better known as sharpshooter Annie Oakley. In one nine-hour contest, she fired at 5,000 targets and hit 4,772 of them, for a consistent ninety-five percent.

————?¿————

Q: Who starred as Annie Oakley in the 1935 movie of the same name?

A: Barbara Stanwick (1907-1990).

————?¿————

Q: What was the claim to fame of Sadie Orchard of Lake Valley, New Mexico, in the 1880s and 1890s?

A: She was New Mexico's only woman stagecoach driver. She and her husband, J. W., owned the Lake Valley, Hillsboro and Kingston Stage and Express Line. She also operated a bordello in Kingston on Virtue Street.

————?¿————

Photo courtesy of the Utah State Historical Society

Q: Pictured here is Harry Longbaugh, the Sundance Kid. Who is the lady in the picture?

A: Schoolteacher Etta Place. She accompanied Longbaugh and Butch Cassidy to South America not long after this picture was taken in 1901. She disappeared from history after 1909 when Longbaugh and Cassidy were allegedly killed at San Vicente, Bolivia.

128

WOMEN OF THE OLD WEST

Q: Who was known as the "Cattle Queen of New Mexico"?

A: Susie McSween Barber (1845-1931). The widow of Alexander McSween (1843-1878) who was killed in the Lincoln County War, she married George Barber in 1880.

———————?———————

Q: What cattle operation did Susie McSween Barber run?

A: She began operation of the Three Rivers Land & Cattle Co. while Barber practiced law in Lincoln and White Oaks. They divorced in 1892. She sold the ranch in 1902 and moved to White Oaks where she lived the rest of her life. She is buried there.

———————?———————

Q: Who was responsible for construction of the convent at the northwest corner of the plaza in Old Albuquerque in the early 1880s?

A: Sister Blandina Segale (1850-1941), a member of the Sisters of Charity and a native of Genoa, Italy, brought in some of the same workmen who worked on the Santa Fe Cathedral. The Sisters of Charity operated several schools, public and private, in the Albuquerque area.

———————?———————

Q: What territory in the Old West was first in the nation's history to grant women the right to vote?

A: The Wyoming Territorial Legislature granted women the right to vote in 1869. When Wyoming was admitted to the Union in 1890, it became the first state to grant women full suffrage.

———————?———————

Q: What is Wyoming's state motto?

A: "Equal Rights." Wyoming is called the "Equality State."

———————?———————

Photo courtesy of the Wyoming State Museum

Q: In the history of women's rights in the United States, what did this woman, Mrs. Eliza A. Swain, do on September 6, 1870, at Laramie, Wyoming?

A: Seventy years old at the time, Mrs. Swain was the first woman to cast a legal vote in the history of the nation.

Q: History records that the Jaramillo sisters of Taos, New Mexico, Maria Josefa (1827-1868), and Ignacia, were stunningly beautiful women. To whom was Josefa married?

A: Famed frontiersman Christopher "Kit" Carson (1809-1868). They were married in 1845 and they died within one month of each other in 1868. They were the parents of seven children, the youngest of which was born ten days before Josefa died.

————————?¿————————

Q: To whom was Ignacia married?

A: Charles Bent (1799-1847), New Mexico's first civil governor under American occupation in 1846. Ignacia was present when her husband was murdered and scalped at their Taos home during an uprising of Taos Indians in January of 1847.

————————?¿————————

Q: Who were Owl Woman and Yellow Woman?

A: The sisters were Cheyenne Indians. Owl Woman married trader and Indian agent William Bent (brother of Charles Bent) in the middle 1830s. After her death in the late 1840s, William Bent married Yellow Woman.

————————?¿————————

Q: There was a dance hall (hurdy-gurdy) established in the late 1860s, in Helena, Montana, which was known as Chicago Joe's Place. Who was Chicago Joe?

A: Josephine Hensley (1844-1899) arrived in Helena from Chicago in 1867. She operated the dance hall, saloon and brothel until her death.

————————?¿————————

Photo courtesy of the Wyoming State Museum

Q: Ella Watson operated a brothel on the Sweetwater range in Wyoming in the late 1880s. She sometimes took livestock in exchange for her favors. In 1889, Ella and storekeeper, Jim Averell, were taken out of their homes by a local cattleman and his cowboys and hung from the same pine tree. By what other name was she known?

A: Cattle Kate. The cattleman tried to justify hanging her by making her out to be a rustler. Indications are that neither she nor Averell were actually cattle thieves.

Photo courtesy of the Denver Public Library, Western History Department

Q: By what name was Alice Ivers Tubbs (1851-1930) better known?

A: Poker Alice. Married three times, she ran gambling parlors and/or brothels in Arizona, Colorado, Kansas, New Mexico, South Dakota and Texas.

Q: Two young ladies, Annie McDougal and Jennie Metcalf, both of the Indian Territory (now Oklahoma) had brief careers as horse thieves and bootleggers in the early 1890s. By what names are they better known in the popular lore of the Old West?

A: Cattle Annie and Little Britches. Arrested in 1894, they both served sentences in the reformatory at Farmington, Massachusetts, before becoming respectable citizens later in life.

————?————

Q: Who played Cattle Annie McDougal in the movie *Cattle Annie and Little Britches*?

A: Amanda Plumber.

————?————

Q: One of the last stagecoach robbers in the Old West was a woman. She and her partner robbed a coach near Globe, Arizona, in 1899. What was her name?

A: A Phoenix prostitute and opium addict named Pearl Hart and her pimp, Joe Boot.

————?————

Q: Was it a successful robbery?

A: No. They could not afford horses and were both on foot and quickly captured. They were both convicted and sentenced to prison at Yuma, Pearl to five years, Joe to seven. Pearl served two years.

————?————

Q: Who wrote the books, *A Century of Dishonor* and *Ramona*, both published in the 1880s, and both critical of the way in which American Indians had been treated by the U.S. Government?

A: Helen Hunt Jackson (1830-1885).

Photo courtesy of the Denver Public Library, Western History Department

Q: Pictured above is Margaret "Maggie" Tobin, born in Missouri in 1867. By what name was she better known to Denver, Colorado, society after 1912?

A: The Unsinkable Molly Brown. She was married to miner Jim Brown who struck it rich in 1894. She changed her name to the more stylish "Molly" and became a figure in Denver, Colorado, society.

Q: How did Molly Brown come to be called Unsinkable?

A: She was aboard the Titanic when it sank in 1912. She became a heroine by nursing some of the injured survivors. She described herself as "unsinkable."

———————?*ι*———————

Q: Who played the title role in the 1964 movie, *The Unsinkable Molly Brown*?

A: Debbie Reynolds.

———————?*ι*———————

Q: By what name was Myra Belle Shirley better known in and around the Indian Territory in the 1880s?

A: Belle Starr (1848-1889). She had liaisons with many lovers. She bore children fathered by outlaws Cole Younger and Jim Reed. She took the name by which history has known her from her short-lived marriage to a Cherokee Indian named Sam Starr.

———————?*ι*———————

Q: Under what circumstances did Belle Starr meet her demise?

A: Very suspicious circumstances. She was shot to death from ambush. Some said her son, eighteen-year-old Ed Reed, killed her. No one was ever convicted of the crime.

———————?*ι*———————

Q: Carry Nation (1846-1911) began her career as an anti-saloon temperance leader with an attack on a saloon in Kiowa, Kansas, in June of 1900. What did she use to smash liquor bottles, mirrors and windows?

A: Bricks and rocks she had gathered in her own backyard. She didn't begin using a hatchet until sometime later.

———————?*ι*———————

Photo courtesy of the Utah State Historical Society

Q: This woman claimed, at various times, to have been an army scout, Pony Express rider, mule skinner, bullwhacker, and wagon train boss. What was her name?

A: Martha Jane Cannary (1848-1903), better known as Calamity Jane. History supports very few of her claims.

Q: Name the unlikely actress who played the title role in the 1953 movie, *Calamity Jane*.

A: Doris Day.

———————?————————

Q: Where was Calamity Jane buried?

A: Legend has it that she was at the card table when Wild Bill Hickok was shot to death in 1876. She was buried next to him in the cemetery at Deadwood, South Dakota, upon her death in 1903.

———————?————————

Q: What was the name of the young woman whose life was spared by Gen. Antonio Lopez de Santa Anna after the Battle of the Alamo in March, 1836, so that she might take word of the massacre to Sam Houston?

A: Susannah Dickerson (or Dickinson) was the widow of Almeron Dickerson, a blacksmith who was killed at the Alamo. She was herself shot in the leg but survived and carried word to Houston.

———————?————————

Q: What happened to Mrs. Zerelda Samuel on January 26, 1875 at her home near Kearney, Missouri?

A: Her son Archie was critically injured (he later died) and her own right arm was so badly smashed when a bomb exploded in her fireplace that it was later amputated.

———————?————————

Q: Why did it happen?

A: Mrs. Samuel was the mother of Frank and Jesse James. Pinkerton agents said later they were only trying to capture the outlaw brothers and the bomb blast was an accident.

———————?————————

LITERATURE AND ART OF THE OLD WEST

Painting & Poetry, Tall Tales & Movies

C H A P T E R   1 0

Q: What artist did an oil painting called *Cavalry Charge on the Southern Plains* (1907)?

A: Frederic Remington (1861-1909). The painting is now in the Metropolitan Museum of Art in New York City.

————?ι————

Q: What sculptor did a famed bronze piece called "The Bronco Buster"?

A: The same Frederic Remington.

————?ι————

Q: Name the author who wrote stories set in California mining towns such as Poker Flat, Sandy Bar and Roaring Camp in the middle nineteenth century.

A: Bret Harte (1836-1902). Two of his best known stories were "The Luck of Roaring Camp" (1868) and "The Outcasts of Poker Flat" (1881).

Q: Sam Clemens contributed a series of letters to the Virginia City (Nevada) *Territorial Enterprise* beginning in 1861. What pseudonym did he use?

A: "Josh."

———————?ₑ———————

Q: Sam Clemens became a reporter for the *Territorial Enterprise* in 1862. What pseudonym did he use then?

A: Mark Twain.

———————?ₑ———————

Q: Who, along with his brother, ventured to the far west and later wrote a book about his travels called *Roughing It*, first published in 1872?

A: Sam Clemens and his brother Orion made the trip in 1861. The book is a mixture of truth and tall tale.

———————?ₑ———————

Q: What character in the literature of the Old West uttered the famous line, "When you call me that, smile!"

A: A Wyoming cowboy in *The Virginian: A Horseman of the Plains*. In chapter two of the novel, the Virginian said it to a man named Trampas who had called him a son-of-a---- during a poker game.

———————?ₑ———————

Q: Who wrote *The Virginian*?

A: Owen Wister (1860-1938) of Philadelphia. It was first published in 1902.

———————?ₑ———————

Q: Who played the Virginian in the 1929 movie of the same name? Who played Trampas?

A: Gary Cooper (1901-1961) played the Virginian. Walter Houston (1884-1950), in his first movie role, played Trampas.

———?ₑ———

Q: The 1962-1969 TV series, *The Virginian*, bore no relationship to Wister's novel. Who played Trampas?

A: Doug McClure.

———?ₑ———

Q: Name the Montana cowboy/artist who did an oil painting called *In Without Knocking* which depicts five armed cowboys trying to ride their horses into a frontier hotel and gambling parlor.

A: Charles Marion Russell (1864-1926). It hangs in the Amon Carter Museum of Western Art in Fort Worth, Texas.

———?ₑ———

Q: What western symbol did Charles M. Russell draw near his signature on his paintings?

A: A cow or buffalo skull.

———?ₑ———

Q: Who wrote *Rawhide Rawlins* and its sequel, *More Rawhides,* and had them privately published in Montana before his death in 1926?

A: The same Charles M. Russell.

———?ₑ———

Q: *The Oxbow Incident* was written by Walter Van Tilburg Clark and published in 1940. What was the "incident"?

A: The lynching of three men -- innocent, as it turned out -- for cattle rustling.

———?ₑ———

Q: Who starred in the 1943 William Wellman movie, *The Ox-Bow Incident*?

A: Henry Fonda and Harry Morgan played a couple of cowboys who failed to prevent the lynching of three supposed rustlers played by Anthony Quinn, Dana Andrews and Francis Ford.

————?*l*————

Q: Who wrote *The Authentic Life of Billy the Kid* which was published in Santa Fe in 1882?

A: It was ostensibly written by Sheriff Pat Garrett (1850-1908) in the months following Billy's death at his hands.

————?*l*————

Q: Who really wrote *The Authentic Life of Billy the Kid*?

A: It is generally believed that an itinerant newspaperman, postmaster and justice of the peace, named Marshall Ashmun "Ash" Upson (1828-1894) actually did the writing for Garrett.

————?*l*————

Q: Who wrote the 1881 novel, *The True Life of Billy the Kid*?

A: John Woodruff Lewis. This effort was published by the Wide Awake Library (a five cent novel publisher in New York City) less than six weeks after Billy was killed in Fort Sumner, New Mexico, on July 14, 1881.

————?*l*————

Q: Who wrote the 1926 book, *The Saga of Billy the Kid*?

A: Walter Nobel Burns claimed historical accuracy but was more often than not short of the notch.

————?*l*————

Q: Who did an oil painting called "Self-Torture in the Mandan Okipa Ceremony" in 1832?

A: George Catlin (1796-1872). This painting inspired the self-torture scene in the 1969 movie *A Man Called Horse* starring Richard Harris.

———?———

Q: Who wrote the western novels *Shane* and *Monte Walsh*?

A: Jack Schaefer. When he wrote *Shane* in 1946, he had never been west of Cleveland, Ohio. He moved to Cerrillos, New Mexico, in 1954. He died there in 1991 at the age of eighty-three.

———?———

Q: Who played the title role in the 1953 movie *Shane*, considered by many to be one of the very best westerns ever made?

A: Alan Ladd (1913-1964). It was certainly Ladd's best role.

———?———

Q: Who played the title role in the 1970 movie *Monte Walsh*?

A: Lee Marvin (1924-1987).

———?———

Q: Who played the title role in the 1983 movie, *The Ballad of Gregorio Cortez*?

A: Edward James Olmos.

———?———

Q: Who directed John Wayne's classic 1949 western film, *She Wore a Yellow Ribbon*?

A: John Ford (1895-1973).

———?———

Q: Who wrote a series of articles for *Galaxy* magazine between 1872 and 1874, later published in book form, called *My Life on the Plains*?

A: Gen. George Armstrong Custer.

————————?ɩ————————

Q: Name the Texas and New Mexico lawman who wrote a book in 1948 (when he was 83 years old) called *Mean as Hell*?

A: Daniel R. (Dee) Harkey served as a lawman in Texas before moving to Eddy County, New Mexico, in 1890 where he served as a lawman from 1893 to 1911. He claimed to have been shot at more times than any man in the world not engaged in a war.

————————?ɩ————————

Q: What famous and best selling novel was written by New Mexico Territorial Governor (1878-1881) Lew Wallace (1827-1905) and published in 1880?

A: *Ben Hur.*

————————?ɩ————————

Q: Who wrote *Death Comes for the Archbishop* (1926), a novel based on the life of Jean Baptist Lamy (1814-1888) who was Archbishop of Santa Fe from 1875 to 1888?

A: Willa Cather (1876-1947).

————————?ɩ————————

Q: Who wrote *O Pioneers!*, a book about the tribulations of farm life in early Nebraska?

A: Willa Cather, born in Virginia, reared in Nebraska.

————————?ɩ————————

Q: Who wrote a book in 1947 about the fur trade in the Rocky Mountains and along the Missouri River in the 1830s called *The Big Sky*?

A: A. B. Gutherie, Jr. (1901- --).

————————?ɩ————————

Q: Who starred in the 1952 Howard Hawks movie *The Big Sky?*

A: Kirk Douglas and Arthur Hunnicutt.

————?¿————

Q: A young writer named Frank Norris (1870-1902) wrote a book about California farmers and their fight with the railroads. What was it entitled?

A: *The Octopus: A Story of California* was published in 1901.

————?¿————

Q: Who played Will Kane in the 1952 western movie classic *High Noon?*

A: Gary Cooper (1901-1961) won an academy award for best actor for his portrayal of the marshal of Hadleyville.

————?¿————

Q: Francis Parkman (1823-1893) journeyed from St. Louis, Missouri, to Fort Laramie, Wyoming, in 1846. Name the book he wrote about his trip?

A: *The Oregon Trail* was published in 1849.

————?¿————

Q: Dan De Quille was a *nom de plume* used by what editor of the Virginia City (Nevada) *Territorial Enterprise* from the 1860s to the 1890s?

A: William Wright (1829-1898), a native of Iowa, spent nearly forty years in Virginia City. He was well-acquainted with young Sam Clemens who also worked for the *Territorial Enterprise* in the early 1860s.

————?¿————

Q: Who wrote *No Life For a Lady*, a book about New Mexico ranch life at the turn of the century?

A: Agnes Morley Cleaveland (1874-1938).

Q: Who created the fast-shooting fictional character, "The Cisco Kid"?

A: William Sydney Porter (1862-1910), better known as O. Henry. One source says noted Texas killer John Wesley Hardin was the model upon which the Cisco Kid was based.

————————?¿————————

Q: What was the real name of dime novelist Ned Buntline?

A: Edward Zane Carroll Judson (1823-1886).

————————?¿————————

Q: Who played the part of Ned Buntline in the 1976 movie, *Buffalo Bill and the Indians or Sitting Bull's History Lesson*? Who played Buffalo Bill Cody?

A: Burt Lancaster played Buntline. Paul Newman played Cody.

————————?¿————————

Q: What American writer went to Mexico during Pancho Villa's Revolution in the fall of 1913 and disappeared from the pages of history after December 26 of that year?

A: Ambrose Bierce, born in 1842. He was the author of *The Devil's Dictionary*, which held that self-esteem was an erroneous appraisement.

————————?¿————————

Q: *The Scouts of the Prairie and Red Deviltry as It Is*, a melodrama, was written by Ned Buntline. It opened in Chicago in late 1872. Critics and audiences of the time both declared it among the worst melodramas ever staged. Who starred in it?

A: Buffalo Bill Cody played himself, as did Texas Jack Omohundro. Buntline played Gale Berg and the damsel in distress, Dove Eye, was played by Giuseppina Morlacchi.

Q: Who played the lead in the 1944 movie, *Buffalo Bill?*

A: Joel McCrea (1905-1990).

————?¿————

Q: What author wrote *The Last of the Plainsmen* (1908), *Riders of the Purple Sage* (1912) and many other western stories?

A: Zane Grey (1875-1939) of Zanesville, Ohio.

————?¿————

Q: What historian wrote the following in a paper called "The Significance of the Frontier in American History" in 1893?

To the frontier the American intellect owes its striking characteristics. That coarseness and strength combined with acuteness and inquisitiveness; that practical, inventive turn of mind, quick to find expedients; that masterful grasp of material things, lacking in the artistic but powerful to effect great ends; that restless nervous energy; that dominant individualism working for good or evil and withal that buoyancy and exuberance which comes with freedom -- these are the traits of the frontier.

A: Frederick Jackson Turner (1861-1932). His thesis maintained that the American character was defined by the frontier rather than by an amalgam of European cultural influences.

————?¿————

Photo by Gloria Bullis

Writer Don Bullis is pictured here visiting the grave of Sheriff Pat Garrett at Las Cruces, New Mexico.

Don Bullis graduated from Eastern New Mexico University at Portales in 1970 with a Bachelors Degree in History and English. In the years since, he has worked as a small-town New Mexico newspaper editor and columnist and as a deputy sheriff and town marshal. He is currently a special agent for the New Mexico Department of Public Safety, Special Investigations Division. He is also working on two other books. He and his wife Gloria live in Rio Rancho, New Mexico.

BIBLIOGRAPHY

Benton, Frank. *Cowboy Life on the Sidetrack*. Denver: Western Stories Syndicate, 1903.

Betenson, Lula Parker. *Butch Cassidy, My Brother*. Provo: Brigham Young University Press, 1975.

Bethune, Martha Fall. *Race With the Wind, The Personal Life of Albert B. Fall*. El Paso: A Novio Book, 1989.

Bullis, Don. *New Mexico's Finest: Peace Officers Killed in the Line of Duty 1874-1989*. New Mexico Department of Public Safety, 1990.

Clark, Neil M. (ed.). *Campfires and Cattle Trails, Recollections of the Early West in the Letters of J. H. Harshman*. Caldwell: Caxton Printers, 1970.

Clark, Walter Van Tilburg. *The Oxbow Incident*. New York and Toronto: The New American Library, 1940.

Custer, George Armstrong. *My Life on the Plains*. New York: The Citadel Press, 1962.

Daniel, Clifton (ed.). *Chronicle of America*. Paris: Jacques Legrand, 1989.

Ewers, John C. *Artists of the Old West*. Garden City: Doubleday & Co., 1965.

Fugate, Francis and Roberta. *Roadside History of New Mexico*. Missoula: Mountain Press Publishing Company, 1989.

Garrett, Pat F. *The Authentic Life of Billy the Kid*. Norman: University of Oklahoma Press, 1954.

Gibson, A. M. *The Life and Death of Colonel Albert Jennings Fountain*. Norman: University of Oklahoma Press, 1965.

Graham, W. A. *The Custer Myth, A Source Book of Custeriana*. New York: Bonanza Books, 1953.

Harkey, Dee. *Mean as Hell: The Life of a New Mexico Lawman*. Santa Fe: Ancient City Press, 1989.

Harrison, Fred. *Hell Holes and Hangings*. Clarendon: Clarendon Press, 1968.

Horgan, Paul. *Great River, The Rio Grande in North American History*. Austin: Texas Monthly Press, 1954.

Hornung, Chuck. *The Thin Gray Line: The New Mexico Mounted Police*. Fort Worth: Western Heritage Press, 1971.

Katz, William Loren. *The Black West, A Documentary and Pictorial History*. Garden City: Anchor Press/Doubleday, 1973.

Keleher, William A. *The Fabulous Frontier*. Albuquerque: University of New Mexico Press, 1962.

Kelly, Charles. *The Outlaw Trail, A History of Butch Cassidy and His Wild Bunch*. New York: Bonanza Books, 1959.

Leckie, William H. *The Buffalo Soldiers, A Narrative of the Negro Cavalry in the West*. Norman and London: University of Oklahoma Press, 1967.

Long, Jeff. *Duel of Eagles*. New York: William Morrow and Company, Inc., 1990.

Martin, Mick, and Marsha Porter. *Video Movie Guide, 1992*. New York: Ballantine Books, 1991.

Maule, Harry E. (ed.). *Great Tales of the American West*. New York: The Modern Library, 1945.

BIBLIOGRAPHY

Metz, Leon G. *Pat Garrett: The Story of a Western Lawman*. Norman and London: University of Oklahoma Press, 1973.

Monaghan, Jay, (ed.). *The Book of the American West*. New York: Julian Messner, Inc., 1963.

Moody, Ralph. *The Old Trails West*. Promontory Press, 1963.

Nash, Jay Robert. *Bloodletters and Badmen*. New York: M. Evans and Company, Inc., 1973.

Parkman, Francis. *The Oregon Trail*. Garden City: Doubleday & Company, 1946.

Parsons, Chuck. *Clay Allison: Portrait of a Shootist*. Seagraves: Pioneer Book Publishers, 1983.

Pearce, W. M. *The Matador Land and Cattle Company*. Norman: University of Oklahoma Press, 1964.

Rand McNally Contemporary World Atlas. Chicago/New York/San Francisco: Rand McNally & Company, 1986.

Reedstrom, Ernest L. *Scrapbook of the American West*. Caldwell: Caxton Printers, Ltd., 1991.

Rollins, Philip Ashton. *The Cowboy, An Unconventional History of Civilization on the Old-Time Cattle Range*. New York: Ballantine Books, 1973.

Simmons, Marc. *On The Santa Fe Trail*. University Press of Kansas, 1986.

— *Ranchers, Ramblers and Renegades: True Tales of Territorial New Mexico*. Santa Fe: Ancient City Press, 1984.

Stafford, Harry Errald. *The Early Inhabitants of the Americas*. New York: Vantage Press, 1959.

Time-Life Books. Eds. *The Old West*. Alexandria: 1974.

Utley, Robert M. *Frontier Regulars, The United States Army and the Indian, 1866-1891*. Lincoln and London: University of Nebraska Press, 1973.

— *High Noon in Lincoln: Violence on the Western Frontier*. Albuquerque: University of New Mexico Press, 1987.

Webb, Walter Prescott. *The Texas Rangers: A Century of Frontier Defense*. Austin: University of Texas Press, 1987.

White, Richard. *It's Your Misfortune and None of My Own*. Norman and London: University of Oklahoma Press, 1991.

Wister, Owen. *The Virginian*. New York: Pocket Books, 1956.

INDEX

INDEX

INDEX

INDEX

154

INDEX

INDEX

INDEX

INDEX

INDEX

INDEX